A Maze
of
Twisty Passages

A Maze
of
Twisty Passages

The life of a student in 1970s Cambridge
and
what came next

Judy Holyer

ISBN 13: 9781790152728

Contents

1. Setting Out

Thirty women. Three hundred and thirty men. This was the good life. I could take my pick. It was October 1972 and I was ready for this new phase of my life. I had just arrived at Churchill College, Cambridge as one of its first female undergraduates, eager to get down to some serious mathematical study.

I enjoy language. I read books. I look at signs and revel in their unintended ambiguity. 'This door is alarmed.' Poor door, who frightened it? Why on earth would anybody build a disabled toilet? I want one that works. What is the difference between a 'Gender-neutral Toilet' and an ordinary everyday toilet that anyone can use. When I am driving, am I really supposed to 'Use Both Lanes'? Do 'Free Range Eggs' enjoy their short lives gambolling around fields? I did once start a report with the phrase, 'In this article we will look at how members of churches are broken down by age and sex.' I do not know how I got away with that one. Perhaps, when I was younger, it was the lack of precision in language that attracted me to mathematics. I wanted a bit of security. I wanted a subject with correct answers that did not interfere with my everyday life. It took me a while to realise that mathematics has its ambiguities too. I could not have studied theology at seventeen. It would have upset my world; turned my life upside down. But more of that later.

This is a book about myself and my life but, in some sense, it is true of all books that they are about the author. It is good to think that I can be the author of my own life. I would like it to be an objective story, keeping to facts, but life is a subjective experience. There is no objective position in which to stand. This is my life as I have known it. It is hard to start writing and I know all the strategies to avoid getting down to the task at hand. I have known too many students and have heard all the excuses. I have been intending to place some words on paper for at least ten years; maybe, even to write a book. However, until recently, I had not been able to focus on exactly what I wanted to write or who might be interested in my ramblings. My previous writing has either been articles for academic journals or sermons. Now I am ready to start. I hope.

As I get older I realise that I need to write down some recollections of my life if they are not to be forgotten. My experience of life seems to have become 'history'. I have been a 'first' woman in a number of ways. I was the first woman in my family to go to university. I was one of the first women to go to Churchill College. I got a first class degree in mathematics. I was my research supervisor's first female Ph.D. student. I lectured in a university maths department where I was one of two women out of more than thirty staff and was the only person under thirty. I was ordained as a Baptist minister two years before women were ordained in the Church of England. I was the only woman director out of thirteen people on the board of the IT company that three colleagues (male, of course) and I set up in 1999. I wonder if people might be interested in my life. I will only ever find out if I tell my story. It is my story, endlessly fascinating to me as I continue to learn more about myself. It is something I must write for myself. I expect to be forgotten by most people but I have a fantasy of a record of my life gathering dust in Churchill College Archives Centre, along with the likes of Winston Churchill, Margaret Thatcher, John Major, Frank Whittle and Rosalind Franklin. All that really matters to me is that I have lived and that I continue to live until I die. What happens after that is a closed book.

Setting Out

I remember the archives centre being built, back in 1972. It feels to me as if my life began in the October of that year when I went to Churchill. Just seventeen years old, I came from Llwyn-y-bryn Senior Comprehensive Girls' School in Swansea. I did baulk at being a comprehensive girl and renamed the school on my UCCA form as Llwyn-y-bryn Senior Comprehensive School for Girls. I was not initially keen to apply to Cambridge. I only knew of people who had applied and not got in. I wanted to go to Imperial College in London but my parents did not approve of that idea and, in those days, I did as I was told. My parents wanted me to go to Bristol where my brother, David, was already studying maths but they were happy for me to apply to Cambridge first, although they assumed I would not get in. After all, I was not supposed to be as clever as my brother.

We had moved to Swansea from Hemel Hempstead, Hertfordshire, three years earlier, when my father, a civil servant, moved to work at the DVLC that was just opening as the national centre for driver and vehicle licensing. My father was from South Wales, could speak some Welsh; and was keen to return to Wales. My Welsh pronunciation improved dramatically as I was put in Miss Llewellyn's class in a school with no vowels in its name. It was a shock to me, moving a year before my O-levels from a mixed grammar school only twenty miles from London to a girls' school that had just turned comprehensive. I took up geography, as there was a choice between that and biology, neither of which I had been studying; and I dropped chemistry, which I wanted to continue studying but it clashed with history, which my new headmistress persuaded my father was a much more useful subject for her girls. I found myself in a class where everyone else had taken both English and maths O-level at the end of the fourth form. No-one had got higher than a grade 3 in maths but the class had nevertheless moved on to additional maths so I was put in a lower set. I found myself very bored repeating work I had already covered and managed to move to the additional maths class which was more challenging and enjoyable, as we studied calculus for the first time. At the end of the year the school was stunned when I got two grade 1's in maths and additional maths, as well as 1's in geography, French and German, 2's in physics, Latin and history, a 4 in English literature and a 5 English language. I should add that a grade 1 in those days was a top grade and a bare pass was a grade 6. Most exam boards as that time used letters rather than numbers, but the Welsh board liked to be different. I had been somewhat flummoxed when I saw the history paper which was bilingual and contained rubric that stated that I could answer the questions in either Welsh or English. This was not true. I was not able to answer in Welsh! As I moved into the sixth form, I wanted to take German and double maths at A-level but it was not allowed to mix maths with anything other than a science subject. I ended up doing double maths and physics.

Hemel Grammar had had some sort of link with Churchill College, which put it in my mind when I was asked to apply to Cambridge. There was a maths teacher that I rather liked called Mr Trickett who had been to Churchill. He must have been young as it was only five years since Churchill had been founded, but I did not notice that. What I noticed, in my first year at Grammar school, when I was not yet eleven, was that he encouraged me and gave me confidence to speak up in class when I knew answers to problems. I liked the thought of following in his footsteps. One or two pupils had gone to Churchill too, but I imagined that they were really clever. Even my brother, who is three and a half years older than me, and, according to my parents, much cleverer than me, had not applied to Cambridge. That was partly because we were moving and he would have been required to stay at school for a third year sixth. Instead, he looked for a scholarship and was sponsored through university by the Post Office. He had a brilliant year out before going to Bristol, travelling around various Post Office locations including the telecommunications research centre at Dollis Hill in north west London, where Tommy Flowers had designed and built the Colossus computer with 1800 vacuum tubes to assist the wartime decoding work at Bletchley Park. My brother had all his fees and living expenses paid throughout his course, as well as interesting vacation work. I did not apply for anything similar. Few scholarships were open to women and I wanted to go straight to university without taking a year out.

I browsed through the prospectus and pored over colleges. I saw Churchill was just going mixed which encouraged me. I could not bear the thought of three years living in an exclusively female environment. I had only just discovered how bitchy girls can be. Churchill also took 70% scientists and I thought that might give me a better chance of getting in. I liked its modern architecture, which I would never call brutalist. However, I discovered that it was a requirement to be eighteen years old to go up to Cambridge. I had always been a year ahead at secondary school so I would only be seventeen when I went to university unless I had a year out. I went to see Miss Havill, my headmistress, to tell her that I could not apply to Cambridge because I was too young. She took it in her stride. She thought it an admirable idea to apply to a mixed college as my grant would go further, with the young men thronging to take me out, and she would write to the college immediately to see if they would allow me to apply despite my age. She received a letter from, I think, a Mr Tizard, who said that I could apply and take the entrance exam. Then if I did well enough they would interview me to decide whether I was sufficiently mature to come in 1972 or whether I should wait a year. I did decide to apply although I never found my grant went further! My headmistress had obviously never heard of going Dutch. Perhaps that is why she had never found a husband, despite years of flirting with fathers of pupils.

None of the teachers at my school could do the entrance exam questions. At least, they could only do the questions that I could do without their help. After attending both single sex school and mixed schools, my experience was that girls were discouraged from taking science in the mixed school but the teaching of science was not good in the girls' school. Both of these phenomena led to fewer girls studying science subjects than arts subjects. I had some useful help in the entrance exam from Dr Ken Chandler, a colleague of my father's at the DVLC. He had a Ph.D. in statistics from the University of Nottingham. A life-long bachelor; we had a few awkward sessions in his bungalow where he showed me how to do some of the questions on probability and statistics. I became expert at pulling imaginary coloured socks out of drawers and tossing coins. He was not used to female company and I had never before met someone with a Ph.D. but we struggled along and it was thanks to him that I did as well as I did in the entrance exam.

Indeed, I must have done well because when a letter arrived from the college it offered me a place for immediate entry, subject to getting two A-levels at any grade and on passing the Use of English exam. The letter arrived on a Saturday morning when my parents were out shopping and I was home alone. The letter was thin so I assumed it was the rejection letter that I had been led to expect. It was never checked that I was mature enough which was probably just as well, as while I was academically able, I was young, emotionally immature, and unconfident. When my parents got home I told them that Churchill was not inviting me for interview. My mother's reaction was to say 'Never mind. It doesn't matter.' On hearing that I had been offered a place without interview she immediately started to phone friends and relations to pass on the good news, as if it was her achievement not mine. She never once congratulated me. But that did not matter. I would be able to get away from her. Cambridge is about as far east as you can travel from Swansea without ending up in the North Sea.

I was worried about the Use of English exam and kept hold of my offer to Bristol where I was asked for a grade A and two B's in pure maths, applied maths and physics. It seemed to me that it might be a better prospect than passing Use of English. I was worried because the only books that I read in the sixth form were science fiction but the exam had an essay title, 'Let the sunshine in.' I did not recognise the quote, but managed to write a dystopian piece on the end of life on Earth as the sunlight faded due to some unexplained cause. I had also applied to Nottingham but had been prevented from getting to their interview by fog. At Swansea University I was interviewed by a lecturer who just seemed to assume that I would be going to Cambridge. He asked if I knew how to prove that the square root of 2 is irrational. I said yes. I was not asked how to prove it but was then asked if I knew how to prove that π is irrational. I said I did not. That answer got me the offer of a place as he recognised the astuteness of my two answers. I knew that it is hard to prove π irrational (and even harder to prove it transcendental). I was very keen not to go to the same university as my brother and my anxiety levels were high by the summer of 1972. I always feared failing exams. It was with much relief that I did pass the Use of English, the world did not end, and my place was confirmed.

I had not felt the pressure with the entrance exam because there was no expectation that I would pass. Four of us from the school took the Oxbridge exams; one for English at Oxford, two for Natural Sciences at Cambridge, and myself for Mathematics. Two of us got places. Noreen Thomas went to Newnham College to read Natural Sciences. It was a very good year for the school which rarely had any Oxbridge success and it was almost despite our schooling that we got places. In the first year sixth the school was closed for six weeks due to a council workers' strike and no work was organised for us until the fourth week when we were given some past A-level papers to work on. The school's applied maths teacher had left just before my first year sixth to go to Mynydd Bach, another unpronounceable comprehensive girls' school in Swansea. There was a group of about ten taking the pure and applied maths single A-level and for reasons beyond my understanding we rushed through the syllabus so that everyone could take the A-level at the end of the first year sixth. That was fine for me but most of the others resat the paper for better grades the following year. The pure maths teacher taught the applied maths as well in my first year sixth which was a new venture for him and he kept a page ahead of us in the textbook. I kept a page ahead of him. I had learnt early on in my secondary education not to answer questions or volunteer anything in lessons after a maths teacher in my second year told me to put my hand down after he asked a question. He said everyone in the class knew that I knew the answer and was there anyone else who could answer. I never spoke again in maths lessons. I got bored and it must have given the impression that I did not really understand, because at the end of the fourth form, when I left the school, there was a parents' day at which they were told that I would be OK for maths O-level but would not be good enough for A-level. I think that school was prejudiced against girls doing maths and encouraged them to do something else if there was anything else that they were good at and I was top of the class in everything but physical education. The result was that when I reached the maths A-level class in the sixth form I was not at all confident of my abilities and when I noticed the teacher make a mistake in the problem he was doing on the board I said nothing. He got to the end and, unsurprisingly, did not get the correct answer. He asked us if we could see where he had gone wrong and after some awkward minutes I pointed out his error, early on in the calculation. I learnt then that it might have been better to say something earlier. It did have the effect that when I started to lecture I went to some lengths not to embarrass students and to encourage them to ask about anything that they did not understand or follow. There were three of us doing pure maths A-level which with the teacher made the perfect number for playing solo whist. The cards were rapidly hidden whenever we heard someone outside, especially if it was the headmistress. And we did work through some past papers. We all got a grade A, which was put down to my influence. An applied maths teacher, straight out of college, was appointed for the beginning of my second year sixth. I was her only A-level student but she still used to stand at the board and get me to take notes. It felt very odd with just the two of us in a large classroom. She was a good teacher and tried to help with the entrance exams. It was only after I got a place that she told me that her brother was studying Russian at Churchill College, though was currently in Moscow on his year abroad. Her name was Miss Jones, a good Welsh name, and I met her brother, Dafydd, later when he was back at Churchill for his final year.

I was shocked and very pleased at the offer of a place at Cambridge but apprehensive at what life would be like. I took up the offer to visit the college in the spring of 1972 and met with Dr John Knott, a metallurgist, who was to be my personal tutor, and with Dr Graham Dixon, who was the director of studies in mathematics. I was very intimidated on my first visit. I liked John Knott. He was very friendly and supportive. Graham Dixon was more like Ken Chandler, somewhat reserved and distant. I was not reassured that I would survive in an environment where everyone would be cleverer than me.

Before term started I received a guide for new students. Clearly edited from an earlier version dating from the single-sex days of the college, it aimed to be gender neutral but had an unusual stilted style in which it referred to the student as he/she and had a contrived section on his/her guests who were referred to as she/he. At least it did manage to avoid referring to girls and men, which was a tendency of the time. The college still had gate hours and the gate by the porters lodge was closed at 2am every night, by which time guests were expected to have left. My mother's comment was that anything could have happened by 2am, which was certainly true, and she did not know that it was always possible to go in and out via the playing fields or even through the porters' lodge for those who felt more blatant. Of course, some students did have guests staying overnight and, early on, I was told of one student who, prior to the arrival of female students in college, had installed a double bed in his room instead of the single one supplied. Apparently women were seen in breakfast both before and after the college went mixed. In my first year all students were placed on single sex staircases. Later there was an option to live on mixed staircases though I never took that up. I was quite happy not sharing toilets and showers with men. The guide did tell me that we could affix posters to our walls with the new invention of blu tack, which would not mark the walls. This led me to travel to Cardiff where I managed to find some at a shop selling posters, after a few looks of bewilderment when I enquired about it. I came away with the 1968 Christmas Eve Apollo 8 photo of the earth from the moon, known as Earthrise, which graced my walls for all my undergraduate years at Churchill, by which time I had established that blu tack did damage paint and the college had banned it.

2. Part IA

So October 1972 arrived and my parents drove me and my belongings to Cambridge. It was a long cross-country trip over the heads of the valleys road, past Tewkesbury, through the Cotswolds, past the concrete cows of Milton Keynes and John Bunyan's statue in Bedford and then onto the A1 at the Black Cat Roundabout from where it was just a short distance through St Neots and down the Madingley Road to reach college. My mother was very keen to come to see where I would be studying. When we found the staircase, my name, J.Y. Probert, was already on the board of names, which made me feel like a real student. I did not have much in the way of belongings. Apart from a few clothes, I had an electric kettle, a purple Bang and Olufsen radio and my poster of Earthrise. By the end of the first term I had acquired lots of books and other bits and pieces but had to return to Swansea by train. I had two suitcases so filled one with clothes and the other with books. That seemed logical to me. It was the dim and distant days before there were wheels on suitcases so I only made that mistake once. I struggled across London from Liverpool Street to Paddington and arrived back in Swansea for Christmas with one arm longer than the other.

But back to the beginning of term. I had escaped home and avoided Bristol. I could start to live and breathe. I loved my new study bedroom with its wide granite window seat with two large square cushions, the black square coffee table and the maple floors. I suppose that I should mention the mirror. It was quite well hidden. At the end of the room was what looked liked wooden panelling, which concealed cupboards. One of the cupboards contained a washbasin and the other opened onto a wardrobe with a full length mirror on the inside of the door. I quickly understood that it was only the women's rooms which had these mirrors. Was it a sign that we were supposed to worry about how we dressed? I would have preferred not to have had the mirror. Some of the men were envious and agitated for mirrors of their own. I was most impressed with the anglepoise light on my desk. I had never before seen an adjustable lamp. It looked like a good room to work in and that was how I was planning to spend most of my time. Terms lasted just eight weeks and I could only imagine that there would be a lot of work to fit in. My room, 46B, overlooked the archives centre building site but I enjoyed watching the building work, at least until near the end of the year when, with ear-splitting screeching, they started to cut paving slabs for a path. A bedder came every weekday to make the bed and tidy the room. The rooms had been designed for the conference market and the college was often full of guests in the vacations so it was convenient to have the bedders employed year round. I did discover that the bedders preferred to look after the young men; mothering them, washing up cups and clearing up if there had been a party. The college may have gone mixed but the bedders seemed to think that women should do their own cleaning. Even now, I learnt on my last visit to college, all the bedders are still female although I was pleased to learn that from a female porter who told me she was the first to be appointed ten years ago. All the students, men and women, had equivalent workloads and I could see no reason at all why men would need extra pampering unless it is because they are the weaker sex.

After my room had passed my mother's inspection, I was left on my own with a slight feeling of abandonment. I unpacked and fixed my poster to the wall. I eventually realised that I would have to venture out and meet some other students. It did not occur to me then that most of us would be feeling rather uncertain as to what we should be doing. Altogether in college there were three hundred and sixty undergraduates, and, in this first year of its life as a mixed institution, thirty-four of the undergraduates were women. In 1972 three staircases were allocated to the women and I joined some of them in the staircase kitchen. There we discovered where we were each from, what subject we were reading and where we had been to school; the usual new student stuff. I felt somewhat intimidated by Kari Blackburn who had been to Atlantic College, an independent residential sixth form college, on the coast between Swansea and Cardiff. I think she was planning to study law and had an international baccalaureate. I felt more comfortable with Christine Sinclair from Oldham who was reading Natural Sciences and whose strange Northern accent was outside my experience. I think it was Judy Gunn who was upset at the price of meals in hall and who planned to cook for herself. That first week was full of new experiences.

First there was a photo to be taken of all the new students. We lined up in alphabetical order and stood in rows, tiered so all our faces could be seen. It was taken with an old style camera where we had to stand still for quite some time but everyone behaved and no-one ran from one side to the other to appear twice in the photo. One or two people failed to turn up and their photos were added as passport-like pictures later. It is a real product of the seventies. We are all there with long hair, men and women alike, and not a suit in sight. I ordered a copy from the photographers, Eaden Lilley, mounted on backing board. Some of them were labelled as Churchill College Freshmen 1972 and the others as Churchill College Freshers 1972. I think they were just using old stock and women were expected to opt for the Freshers version. I did not. I was proud to be a Churchill College Freshman. The more recent freshers photos seem more formal than the old ones, with everyone in suits or smart dresses and they seem to be called matriculation photos. I did not hear that word in connection with new students going to university until many years later when I was completing a form that asked for the year in which I matriculated. I assumed it meant the year I graduated because my parents spoke of matriculating at school when they were sixteen having completed their School Certificate. As they did not continue in education I never realised that what they had actually achieved was an exemption to some of the admission requirements for university.

My father took his School Certificate in 1938 and started to study for his Higher School Certificate, taking English and Spanish as main subjects. He left school in early 1939, having passed the civil entrance exam, and moved to London from Pontypridd in the Rhondda valley, where he initially worked as a clerical officer for R.V. Jones, who later established the deciphering facility at Bletchley Park. Jobs were very scarce in South Wales at that time and it was deemed to be a much greater achievement to get a job in London than to stay at school. My mother took her School Certificate in 1940, after the outbreak of war, and she moved to a government admin job until starting to train as a nurse in 1942. My father was billeted over the road from her home in Kenton, North London, and they met while still teenagers. At the start of the war my father was in the home guard, fire watching during the blitz, but then joined the Royal Air Force. He wanted to be a pilot but, probably fortunately for me, they discovered he was colour blind and he was rejected as unfit. He would have been unlikely to survive the war as a pilot, joining up during the Battle of Britain. He never left the country during the war and after basic training got involved in education of new recruits. By 1944 he was teaching Morse code in Blackpool and it was there my parents married in July 1944, when my mother was just 20 and my father 22. Their plan to marry in London was thwarted by the V-1 flying bombs which, one weekend when my mother was away, killed the student nurse in the room adjoining hers. I can only reflect how hard it must have been to reach adulthood during that period.

I was frequently told how lucky I was and I entered university life with enthusiasm. Various groups were looking for likely new recruits. The college boat club was keen to get a women's eight together. I was tempted to try it out but soon realised it meant a lot of early morning starts and blistered hands. I have never been a sporty type and the laddishness of boat club members was anathema to me. I think it did attract people who had rowed at school and who had often been to schools that did not appeal to my more egalitarian instincts. One of the female mathematicians, Helen Swallow, became a keen cox. This had a detrimental affect on her mathematical career.

Early on the Christian Union held tea parties, trying to invite all new students. I recall going with some fear and trepidation to the room of Richard Grant, a 3rd year engineer, where I was offered normal tea, Earl Grey tea or filter coffee, and asked if I wanted to go to some basic bible studies. I did join and coffee became the new addition to my life. Until then I usually drank tea; normal PG Tips, not poncey Earl Grey. I had previously avoided coffee if at all possible. At home it was made with instant coffee boiled up with milk on a cooker and always had a skin on top before it was cool enough to drink. I found it disgusting. When I first smelt filter coffee I realised that I might be missing something. I asked to try some and never looked back. I started to drink it black, as the choice was often between rancid milk and Marvel, instant milk that did not dissolve well. Black coffee became an addiction to the extent that I later got withdrawal symptoms during exams, when I started to shake and get a splitting headache. I did cut back a bit then and started on Earl Grey tea too.

It was not just the coffee that attracted me to the Christian Union in college. It was a varied group and over the years I made many good friends. I was never exactly a 'Jesus Freak' but I was committed in my faith which grew both deeper and broader. In college our bible study groups included Roman Catholics, who were regarded with suspicion by some more evangelical Christians. I did not join the Navigators who had a plan to convert the world and bring about the second coming in a conversion process whereby any convert was supposed to convert two more people until the whole world believed. It focussed very much on discipleship and seemed to take over the lives of those involved. I was more interested in life in all its fullness. I enjoyed Christian Union meetings and attended the CICCU (Cambridge Intercollegiate Christian Union) meetings that were held every Saturday evening in the Cambridge Union building behind the Round Church. I signed up for life membership of CICCU, so I guess that I am still a member. It was interesting that the Christian Union had a preponderance of scientists. I have noticed since then that it is not uncommon for people in the humanities to imagine that science has disproved religion whereas scientists delight in the beauty of the universe, accepting God as a working hypothesis to explain its existence.

Outside college, the main hunting ground for new society members was the freshers' fair, held in the Corn Exchange on the south side of the market square in town. There was a lot of pressure to get people to sign up for three years membership. I avoided all the political groups. I joined the Archimedeans which was the Cambridge University Mathematical Society, the Tensors which was the Churchill and Clare college subgroup of the Archimedeans, the Astronomy club and agreed to attending a taster session of the Go society. I never made it to the Go society. I have forgotten which college their first meeting was to be held in. I set off from college intending to get there but got quite frightened around the market square when I thought someone was following me. I rushed back to college. I did continue with the Astronomical Association by going to their lectures but was more interested in the theory than observing. It did not seem desirable to me to leave the warmth of my bed in the middle of a cold, clear winter's night to cross the college fields to the Madingley Rise telescopes. I was never going to see a black hole or a pulsar that way and that was my interest. There was still hot discussion as to whether black holes actually existed or whether they were just the simplest solution to Einstein's field equations with no physical reality. The mathematics was beyond me then but it was exciting hearing people with more knowledge than me arguing whether or not Cygnus X-1 was a black hole.

I did not have a bike when I arrived at college and everyone else had either brought one with them or was looking to buy one. Lectures were to be a mile and a half away in the Cambridge Philosophical Society in Bene't Street. It was expected that we would cycle there so I phoned my parents and was very pleased when they arranged for the old family bike, an RSW 16 with small fat white wheels, to be sent to me as an unaccompanied package on the train. They were not common as student bikes, indeed, I only recall one other person with one, another mathematician, by the name of Ian Holyer. I could never ride that bike without both hands on the handlebars and signalling to turn right was tricky. It was only later, when I got a replacement bike with full size wheels that I discovered that it was not my lack of skill but the lower angular momentum of the smaller wheels that made it harder to balance.

I was not quite the youngest in the year. That honour fell on Pete Cussons, another mathematician, who was three months younger than me. As a seventeen year old I was uncertain of my legal status in the buttery bar but it did not really matter. I have never been someone to frequent bars and if I wanted to stay financially solvent, I could not afford to spend time, and therefore money, there. Being younger never seemed to be a problem. I had always been a year ahead. It also did not seem to make things any more difficult for me that I was a woman. I had just come from three years at a school where boys were regarded as an exotic species who were to be idolised, adored and loved. That had never seemed natural to me and it was simply a relief to be back in a gender-mixed environment.

Everyone is different and some differences are more visible than others. Gender is just one visible difference. There were two black students in our year at Churchill, both doing maths. Steve Cumberbatch was British and I do not think he found it too hard settling in. The other black student was from Guyana and did find it hard. For quite a while I thought he was African, confusing Ghana in Africa with Guyana in South America. All the time he was in Cambridge he wore an anorak. He found it perpetually cold in a place where the icy wind is said to come straight from the Urals. Initially I was bemused by his name, Halvard White, because he was definitely not white. Eventually I learnt his surname had slave origins. His family was of African descent and had been slaves of a white man. Halvard did not often go to lectures, preferring to learn from books, but nevertheless he did well. He was a very keen musician and often played the organ in chapel, becoming an Associate of the Royal College of Organists. Halvard subsequently received a doctorate from Oxford and now lectures maths at the University of the West Indies in Jamaica. He did not seem to have any close friends in college and was hard to get to know at all. There was no one else from a similar background. More recently, I have discovered that almost all people with the surname Cumberbatch are black, because they took the name of the Cumberbatch family who owned them. I continue to reflect, with some shame, how Britain has benefited from the impoverishment of others, especially as I now live in Guinea Street, Bristol, just along the road from the former homes of slave owners, some of whom were Quakers. I was brought up, as was common at the time, to look down on black immigrants. One of the unseen benefits of being at Cambridge was being able to mix with a diverse group of bright people and to discover how much we can learn from each other. We impoverish ourselves if we impoverish others.

When it comes to differences, there is a temptation to focus on things that are visible, like gender and colour. Sometimes the invisible differences can be harder to live with. Homosexuality did not become legal for men over twenty-one until 1967 in England and Wales and not until the 1980s in Scotland and Northern Ireland. Discrimination was rife. It cost Alan Turing his life in 1954. Perhaps it was easier by the 1970s but it must still have been difficult, especially for those students struggling to find their sexual identity. It was never a problem to me. I have always found it perfectly natural to only be sexually attracted to men! Something that did make a difference to me was my nonconformist background, which did not show. The Book of Common Prayer and Choral Evensong are not part of my cultural heritage, so I was glad to be at a non-denominational college with a chapel that had a wide variety of services. I noted that even if I had been male I would have been unable to attend Cambridge until after the Universities Tests Act of 1871 that allowed access to men who were not members of the Church of England. Gender is just one of many differences between people.

I knew of no deaf or blind students while I was an undergraduate at Cambridge and never saw any wheelchairs, apart from Stephen Hawking's. Later, when I was supervising, I did teach an albino student who was partially sighted and he found it hard getting lecture notes that he could read. At that time there were few concessions for disability. I feel sure that many of my fellow maths students would have had a diagnosis somewhere on the autistic spectrum. Certainly some were very strange, and my prejudice would say that it was especially true of students from Trinity college. I do not know all the struggles people had to deal with at college. I do think being female made me stand out, it was not hard for me to deal with. We are all different in some way.

As term got underway and lectures started I discovered that we were studying things that were completely new to me but were revision to others. The lack of good teaching at my school made me feel very inadequate. All the first term I wondered if I was good enough to be at Cambridge. We were paired up for supervisions and I found myself having sessions twice a week with my partner, John Kelly, who was an exhibitioner, and who seemed to think everything was rather easy. Not to be confused with exhibitionists, exhibitioners have done well in the entrance exam and have just fallen short of becoming scholars. We were regularly set problems to solve before our supervisions and they gave me sleepless nights. But I worked hard. Slowly I got on top of the work. Some people complained about the quality of our lecturers. Our analysis course was taught by Alan Baker, who was a Fields Medallist, the Nobel Prize medal of mathematics. He was a less than inspiring lecturer. I am still astonished that he taught the course without using a single diagram. He taught us about continuous and discontinuous functions and calculus, using Greek symbols, and never once drew a graph. It did teach me the Greek alphabet, which came in handy later when I studied New Testament Greek. At the time it just seemed like an unnecessary complication, although it might have helped Petros Ioannou, a Churchill student from Greece. John Conway was our lecturer in algebra and group theory. He was fascinating to listen to but his lectures were not well organised and he was easily diverted from what he was supposed to be teaching. I did discover through him that I had been misspelling the word 'theorem' for years. He tried to inspire us by showing that a theorem was a thing of god, deriving from the two words 'theo' and 'res', meaning respectively God and thing. I looked at the word that I had just written down, 'thereom', and could not understand what he meant. I consulted a dictionary and found I had been misspelling the word ever since I had first heard it at school. His 'derivation', mixing Greek with Latin, was completely spurious, but it did result in me spelling it correctly in subsequent years. Dr MacFarlane, teaching us vectors and tensors, regularly confused left and right handed coordinate systems, because he was left handed. I was impressed at the quality of teaching because all the lecturers were completely familiar with everything they were teaching. It took me a very long time to realise that they ever made any mistakes.

In the end I think the poor teaching that I had at school might have given me an advantage. For me, from an academic point of view, the first year was by far the hardest. Others, especially those from public schools, found it easy and did well in the first year exams on the basis of very little work. There were over two hundred students in first year maths lectures and some dropped by the wayside. My impression was that some had been coached to get in to Cambridge, with no freedom to organise their own work schedules, so that when they were given free time they could not cope. One member of Churchill was a keen bridge player and did no work at all in his first year. He was never up before midday. When he failed his exams at the end of the year he appealed on the grounds that he was a scholar. He simply expected to pass his exams because he was intelligent, confident and from a good school. He did not return for a second year. By the end of the third year about one hundred and fifty students graduated in maths, a drop from about two hundred and fifty in the first year. Some had changed to other subjects but quite a few had been required to leave. After three years, schooling was no longer affecting how well we each did. There was still some false confidence. I would get depressed coming out of exams when some students, usually from Trinity, would boast about how many questions they had answered, knowing that I had not done nearly as many. Later, when the results came out I would realise that they had been exaggerating their abilities. A first in the first year, second in the second year and third in the third year was not uncommon for those who had been force fed at school.

Lectures followed a regular schedule with two pure courses and two applied, each with three lectures a week, held at the same time each morning; either Monday, Wednesday and Friday, or Tuesday, Thursday and Saturday. Yes, we had Saturday morning lectures. It was very rare for anyone to go home for the weekend and the Saturday lectures were a good incentive to keep us at University. I think it was against regulations to leave the University during full term. It was definitely against regulations to take paid work during term time. We only had to juggle our social lives and academic work. I aimed to work everyday until dinnertime at 6pm, with just Saturday afternoon and Sunday free. I had the impression that this was more than most people but the 1970s was not a time when people liked to admit they were working hard. I never did any academic work in the evenings, on Sundays or in the vacations. I found it counter-productive spending too long sitting at a desk staring at a problem that was intractable and sometimes went for a walk while I pondered how to proceed.

My peregrinations would often take me to a bookshop. At the bottom of Trinity Street, opposite Senate House, was Bowes and Bowes, which now houses the Cambridge University Press bookshop. First opened in 1581, it is possibly the oldest bookshop in the country. On Sydney Street stood Galloway and Porter which its Jewish owners always shut on Saturdays. As well as the science fiction of Robert Heinlein and Larry Niven, I started to read books by other authors; Albert Camus, Franz Kafka, Thomas Mann and (for light relief!) George Eliot. Hermann Hesse's *Glass Bead Game* became a favourite with its study of the ambiguity of intellectual life and during the vacations I worked my way through his oeuvre. But during my first year I was more concerned with my studies and by far the best shop for maths books was Heffers, opposite the Great Gate of Trinity College. I would wander my way up to the right hand side of the balcony where the maths and physics books stood waiting. Relative to novels they were really expensive. In my first term I bought each of the recommended textbooks; Jeffreys and Jeffreys *Methods of Mathematical Physics*, Synge and Griffiths *Principles of Mechanics*, Serge Lang *Linear Algebra*, and Apostol *Mathematical Analysis*, along with a college scarf in pink and brown from Ede and Ravenscroft so I looked liked a proper student. I could barely afford them but I cut back elsewhere. I recall buying coffee mugs for 10p each from the market and made it to the end of the year with change from my grant of £480. The books were not good bedtime reading but were a great help in understanding the lectures. Lagrange's theorem, found in Lang's book, became memorable because it kept emphasising that it is a counting theorem (unusual in group theory) but mostly I just skimmed the books trying to find hints to solve the interminable example sheets that we were set. There are very few maths books that I have read from cover to cover. One of those I have read right through is Lighthill's *Waves in Fluids* where I found what should have been 'incompressible' fluids referred to as 'incomprehensible'. I have sympathy with people who would see all maths books as incomprehensible.

My social life at college developed as I found my feet. Andrew Ellis, one of the mathematicians, was keen to get together a group to play Mah Jongg and eight of us put in two pounds each to buy the necessary set of one hundred and forty-four bamboo tiles from Heffers. The game can be played for money but we just kept score. The rules of the game are quite complicated but I soon became proficient at collecting winds and dragons, bamboos and characters in sequences called chow, pung and kong. I can almost remember who was in the group but other people joined us on many occasions so am not quite sure who were the original 'investors'. We were mostly mathematicians. There was one other woman, Alison Rudd, as well as Ian Holyer, Andrew Ellis, Andrew Wilson and David Wilson, who were not related and myself. The other two might have been Mike Farthing and Nigel Sharp, a physicist also from Swansea. It was a good non-threatening way to make friends. I had not known Nigel in Swansea but his school, Bishop Gore, was the local boys grammar school and was much closer to where we lived than Llwyn-y-bryn. I was glad to meet someone else who knew Swansea. Andrew Wilson was a keen sailor and spent every Wednesday afternoon out at Grafham Water, beyond Huntingdon, in a Laser dinghy. Alison enjoyed Scottish country dancing and was also a member of the Fabian Society. Her father was a lecturer in sociology at the University of Essex and she was more politically aware than most of us, although Mike Farthing was a keen member of the Liberal Party. I inadvertently upset Mike's mother despite never meeting her. Aran jumpers were very popular in the 1970s. I had taught myself to knit by making one in bright yellow while watching the beginning of the Munich

Olympics in 1972. I successfully completed my jumper even though the Olympics closed early after a Palestinian terrorist group killed eleven of the Israeli team. Mike had a similar jumper to mine but in a more sober colour. I noticed a mistake in the cable pattern which I pointed out to him. He would have been wiser not to point it out to his mother who had lovingly knitted it. Of the other members of the group, I initially found Ian Holyer rather intimidating. He had taken part in the International Mathematical Olympiad in Poland in 1972 and was very good at solving esoteric maths problems. He seemed outside my league. Andrew Ellis was a cello player who played in a university orchestra. There were other keen musicians amongst the mathematicians. Tony Jones came from even further west in Wales than me. He hailed from Carmarthen and had been leader of one of the two National Youth Orchestras of Wales, or as he said, 'I was leader of the B orchestra.' I gradually got to know a lot of people in college; people from all sorts of backgrounds, both through the Mah Jongg group and through the Christian Union. I found life at college provided a relaxed environment.

In the evening after the self-service hall dinner I would hang around at the bottom of the stairs, where there were two table football machines, waiting to see who else would turn up. While waiting we would often play a game or two. This was taken quite seriously. I was not proficient at table football. Apparently it was not necessary to kick with the feet but I could not stop myself as I attempted to flick the white balls into the tiny goals. Usually I just let the opponents balls drift casually into the goal as I failed to get my players correctly placed. Eventually we would gravitate to one of our rooms either to play Mah Jongg on the conveniently sized black coffee tables that were in all our rooms or just to sit and drink coffee. Occasionally I found myself wandering around college knocking on friends' doors hoping to find someone who was not either out or working. In the days before mobile phones and emails this was common as the only alternative was notes in pigeon-holes which took some planning. Our conversations tended to be wide-ranging. Some of the natural scientists were studying psychology as one of their three first year subjects, which led to us looking at various optical illusions like the duck-rabbit, the vase between two faces and the impossible triangle, used as the basis of Escher's endlessly rising staircase. It made me somewhat more observant of things around me, although I can still houseboat words in sentences, which can make proof-reading difficult. (The textbook used for the course put the word 'houseboat' spuriously in one of the chapters and later pointed out how generally we do not notice words we are not expecting.) By the second term we were studying special relativity and enjoyed discussing the various paradoxes that the subject raised. Was time-travel really impossible? How fast do you need to run to fit a twenty-foot pole into a ten-foot long barn? It was all everyday conversation.

Some social events were more intimidating and I was not quite sure how to behave. Dick Tizard, the same person who had written to my headmistress, invited all students in smallish groups to sherry parties before formal hall. I felt like a fish out of water but was much more relaxed after a few sherries! I made the mistake of making my regular weekly phone call to my mother after the first of these occasions. I queued for the phones in the foyer of Wolfson Hall and, slightly inebriated, admitted how hard I was finding the work. I was shocked to be asked if I wanted to go home when I just wanted some sympathy and encouragement. I never again called home after drinking and stopped talking to my parents at all about academic work. Formal hall itself was fine. It was held every night although few students went to it frequently. The college fellows sat at high table with the students at one of the tables at right-angles to it. The food was brought to us but was the same food as at self-service hall. Although gowns were worn, there were no obvious social faux pas that could be made. This was not true of the annual Founders Feast at which students and college guests were sat together. At the first of these I found myself sitting next to the Master of Trinity Hall. When he spoke to me, he asked what I was studying. I responded and asked him what he did. I was trying to be polite and friendly. He replied in stentorian tones, 'I am the Master of Trinity Hall,' and turned to the people on his other side saying how women should never have been admitted to the college. I felt then as if I had done something terribly wrong and for later feasts always consulted the seating plan in conjunction with 'Who's Who' before going to dinner. I did not recognise then how rude he had been. I made it to the end of the dinner, wondering how it was that I was left with a knife and fork to eat strawberries and cream. The dinner ended with the customary loyal toast, 'The Queen' and then 'Sir Winston', after which smoking was allowed in hall. Cigar smoking was particularly encouraged, although I never got beyond one puff in all my years at college. Cuban ladies may like to smoke cigars but I had no desire to emulate them. In fact very few students smoked at all in the 1970's, with the link between smoking and lung cancer newly established.

The Mah Jongg group were mostly not involved with the Christian Union or the chapel. For most of the first term I cycled down to Newnham on Sunday mornings and went with Noreen Thomas, from my school in Swansea, to Eden Baptist Church, where a young minister was attracting large numbers of students with solid biblical teaching. It was a bit too solid for me and, as I started to get to know people in college, I went with a group of Churchill students to the Church of the Holy Sepulchre, known as the Round Church, which was the oldest church in Cambridge, dating from around 1130 and pre-dating the university. It was very popular with students and you had to arrive early in order to be able to get into the church and avoid having to go to the hall over the road, where the service was relayed for latecomers. This was my first experience of Anglican worship. At first I would get completely lost as to which page we were on in the service book, which was most often the 1662 Book of Common Prayer. The vicar, Mark Ruston, had an endearing habit of always putting a joke into a sermon. They often did not connect well with the rest of the content but they did cause amusement. Some did connect. 'Throw your sins out into the deepest sea and put up a sign, No Fishing!' was a favourite of mine. I found that image more helpful than that of erring and straying like a lost sheep and following the devices and desires of my own heart. I was pleased as the Book of Common Prayer was phased out and modern English phased in. I bought a copy of The Common Bible when it came out in 1974. While the beauty of Shakespearian English may be widely admired, it has never hit the spot with me. William Tyndale was martyred in the cause of translating the Greek and Hebrew bible texts into what was then modern English. His translation formed the basis for the King James Version of the bible produced in 1606. I feel Tyndale turning in his grave when we do not up-date our language so that it can be understood by all. For me, living a life of faith is about learning how everyone can live well in the twenty-first century. I do not want some nostalgic trip into a romanticized past that has no relevance now.

Looking for something more modern I also attended the college chapel. A chaplain had been appointed to the college before there was a chapel. It had been built after a great furore that had led to the resignation of Francis Crick, one of the discoverers of DNA, from his fellowship, on the grounds that a chapel was not needed in this day and age and it might be more appropriate to have a college brothel. The Master, John Cockcroft, was more supportive as I learnt from his daughter, Mary, now an Anglican priest, when we processed side-by-side at the fiftieth anniversary of the chapel. Money to build the chapel was given generously by Lord Timothy Beaumont and a non-denominational chapel was dedicated in 1967. It has never formally become part of the college and is to be found at the top of the playing fields, well away from the rest of the buildings, managed by the trustees of the Chapel at Churchill College, rather than the college's governing body, presumably with the vain hope that members of college would not realise that faith and science are connected. I loved the chapel, which was built in the round with a 3-D cross hanging over the central space. It had the same concrete and brick finish as the rest of the college and beautiful, brightly coloured abstract stained glass windows that were made by John Piper, who had also designed the glass in Coventry Cathedral.

Communion services were held early on Sunday mornings and I occasionally went to them. The incentive to go was that they were followed by breakfast in the chaplain's rooms, with the best boiled eggs and bread that I ever found in Cambridge. The chaplain, Noel Duckworth was a very keen supporter of the boat club, having coxed the Cambridge University eight for several years, as well as coxing in the 1936 Olympics in Berlin. He was known as a supporter of women's rowing so I do not imagine that his retirement at the end of my first year was anything to do with the presence of women in college! He was a gentleman of the old school, although he was known for being quite vivacious at boat club dinners. I met a new group of people at those services. There was Trevor Cave, a third year engineer and also a cox, Phil Aspinall, a fourth year studying chemical engineering, and I think it was there that I first met The Honourable Christopher Monckton, now Lord Monckton, who studied classics, and has become known as a climate change denier. Chris was a rather larger than life eccentric, who had a deep interest in puzzles. I recall spending time in the bar with him discussing mathematical logic. When he graduated he became editor of the universe, which sounded like a magnificent job, even after I discovered that The Universe is a Roman Catholic weekly newspaper, and he also continued with his interest in games, marketing a number of puzzles, one of which offered a £1,000,000 prize to the first person to solve it. Chris, who went to Harrow, seemed to me to be a stereotypical product of the British public school system, like those to be found in Evelyn Waugh's *Brideshead Revisited*, although my favourite character in that book remains Aloysius, Lord Sebastian Flyte's teddy bear, who always kept his counsel.

I had arrived at college without any cuddly toys. I had had a teddy as a young child but, when its rubber nose had got sticky, it had been taken away from me. A few undergraduates had come with furry animals. I was envious of Jackie Mehra and her lion, Winston. He had a bit of a hard life as other students were inclined to attach his tail to the window latch and dangle him out of the window. During my first Easter vac, my father bought me a very round, cuddly sheep with no tail from the Habitat shop in Bristol. There was no potential for him to be hung out of windows and he led a peaceful existence until he passed away some years later, from stuffing cancer. I named that sheep Maxwell, after James Clerk Maxwell, whose equations we were studying. As time went on I acquired more cuddly toys. I discovered that John Betjeman always travelled with his bear, Archibald Ormsby-Gore, and used that as an excuse for walking around with a teddy of my own until I was over forty. At a conference of Baptist ministers in Oxford in the 1990s I learnt from the principal of Regent's Park College, Paul Fiddes, of a book entitled, *Archie and The Strict Baptists*, by Sir John Betjeman. I found a facsimile copy of his original book with delightful illustrations of the bear. I guess I picked up some eccentricity from Chris Monckton!

Sunday morning chapel services generally followed an Anglican format, with an occasional Roman Catholic mass to which everyone was invited. I was more attracted to the evening services which had a more varied format and very often there were visiting preachers. For the fifth anniversary of the chapel, the Archbishop of York, Donald Coggan, who later became Archbishop of Canterbury came to preach. It really surprised me that such a senior figure in the church would come to my college.

As well as Sunday services, weekly bible study sessions were held in college, run by the Christian Union. For the next few years these became a feature of my life. Churchill College does not admit students to study theology but there were still plenty of members of the C.U. There were always several groups running, with about ten people in each group. In my first year, I got involved in running a basic bible study group with Peter Cottingham, a third year engineer. This gave an opportunity to ask questions about what the bible actually said. Peter was, like my brother, sponsored by the Post Office, which gave us an unexpected connection, as he had met my brother during their pre-university year. Somehow what I remember most of those bible study sessions was talking about Peter's third year engineering project on signal processing. He was looking at data flow in transmission lines. At that time there was a real problem in data being corrupted by travelling over long distances. Computer packets still have a check bit to verify that they have been sent correctly but it is rarely needed now. I really enjoyed thinking then about how zeros and ones can be sent as waves down a wire. No-one had ever suggested that I could have studied engineering, which I had only ever associated with building things.

In those sessions I also met Dave Lever, who then occupied the room below Peter's. Dave was a second year mathematician, always ready to help out a first year who had got stuck on a maths problem. I prefer not to think that is why he became a good friend. He had failed to register that Churchill was going to be mixed and set up C.W.O.C.C, short for Chuck Women out of Churchill College, and he decided that I should be its mascot. It was all taken in good heart, although I think it was a sign that it is not easy to adjust from a single-sex environment to a mixed one, for either men or women. Dave was also a passionate supporter of the Ravenglass and Eskdale Railway, which he referred to as La'al Ratty, and encouraged friends to join their preservation society with the same enthusiasm (and lack of success!) with which he encouraged people to join C.W.O.C.C.

The Saturday evening bible readings in the debating chamber of the Cambridge Union became a feature of life. I was sometimes surprised at how naïve the speakers seemed to be. As far as I was concerned there was no conflict between faith and reason, yet it was common for the evangelical speakers to deny the value of science. It seems a waste of time arguing against the validity of evolution only to replace it with contrived stories about how fossils were created to fool us into thinking the world is older than it is. I believe it is much more amazing to realise that the universe is almost fourteen billion years old and that the account of creation in Genesis is not to be read literally but as the easiest way it could be understood at the time the stories were written. After the talks we would return to college, drink coffee and sing choruses from Youth Praise, accompanied on the guitar by Andy Cliffe, another mathematician who later became my supervision partner.

In February of the second term Graham Dixon, the director of studies, and Andrew Tristram, the pure maths fellow, decided to set us exams so they could see how we were getting on and to give us an experience of university exams before the end of year exams in late May. One cold Sunday morning we traipsed up the field to the sports pavilion to sit two three hours sessions in exam conditions, separated into a pure paper and an applied paper. I had never found exams so difficult. I had always got very stressed before exams, fearing that I would fail, but once I settled down it usually got better. With O and A-level exams I found I finished before the time was up and was fairly confident that my answers were correct. With these new exams there was no prospect of finishing a paper. It was just a matter of working until time was up. Questions were formed of bookwork, something we had previously studied, and then an application of that bookwork in what was known as a rider. I knew the riders were important and that it would not be possible to do more than scrape a pass without being able to solve a number of these new, unseen problems. It was hard. A number of people did not read the questions carefully enough and did not do as well as they should have done. I can still embarrass my husband my mentioning that he confused the intermediate value theorem with the mean value theorem, which now just seems cruel of me! The marked papers were returned to us and I was astonished to discover that despite the fact that I was only aware of how little I could do on the papers I had still achieved A-grades on both of them, which was supposed to approximate to a first class result. Those two exams were really helpful to me. I realised I was doing alright and I started to gain a little confidence, even though I continued to fear that I would fail exams.

Lent term of 1973 provided my introduction to computing in the form of Noddy's computer course, at least that was what we called it. It was an optional basic course in programming in Fortran 66 on the university's IBM 370 mainframe computer located in the Computing Lab on the New Museums Site in the middle of Cambridge. Before we could start we had to learn how to create punch cards and how to input them to the computer, using what was called a cafeteria system, with IBM Job Control Language telling the computer to start and end work. This was challenging but necessary. My everyday language started to include //DD EXEC and /* as I came to grips with this frustrating process. My first program, to type 'Hello World!', was a success. The second program was slightly less successful. The aim was to get the printer to type out a multiplication table and I should have ended up with a 12x12 matrix on a single sheet of paper. If the line printer operator had not stopped the program, I would have acquired 144 pages with a single number on each page as my incorrect format statement had asked for a new page with every number printed. I did find a satisfactory pile of rough paper in my pigeon-hole, along with a shirty note informing me of my error. The paper was really good for doing maths; nice and wide with one blank side and green lines on the other in a perforated fanfold. I found it very useful, as at that time all one really needed to do maths was paper, pen and waste-paper basket. I did not use a computer again in earnest until doing my Ph.D. four years later, when I became one of the largest users in the university running programs back-to-back overnight with jobs taking twenty minutes of CPU time and 240K, which was the maximum we were allowed. I learnt to write very efficient and tight code, which is a skill often now lacking in programmers, since time and space constraints are not as strict. The ultra notebook, on which I am writing this, is far more powerful than the IBM 370 of forty years earlier. I did learn from the Noddy's course to always be careful with format statements and that a computer will always do exactly what you have told it to do, which is not necessarily what you want it to do. The aphorism 'To err is human; to forgive divine' has changed in the minds of both my husband and myself into 'To err is human; to really foul things up takes a computer!'

In the Easter vacation of my first year Churchill C.U. hired two minibuses and drove up to the Lake District picking up people on the way. None of my family had ever been to the Lake District so my parents and brother decided to drive me up there a few days earlier. We stayed at a hotel at Bowness-on-Windermere, before I joined the C.U. at the local youth hostel. I was used to walking in the Brecon Beacons with my father and brother but the Lake District hills were harder work. On a cold spring day my brother and I set off up Coniston Old Man. His photos show me getting further and further behind but we had to rush as the weather was closing in. I recall something approaching terror as we jumped over boulders on Dow Crags. When we finally reached the Post Office in Coniston to be picked up we were freezing from the snow that was now falling heavily. The time with the C.U. was gentler. I liked walking with Jackie Mehra, who had the same idea as me as to what was a sensible pace. There was still some snow lying but we went up Helvellyn and Great Gable, running down the scree to get down quickly, and we walked around Ullswater admiring the daffodils that were fluttering and dancing in the breeze. We surprised the congregation at Patterdale Church by doubling its size. It is a beautiful part of the country with no slag heaps to spoil the views from the mountain tops. Dave Lever did not come with us so we did not get to the Ravenglass and Eskdale railway. Nevertheless it is the Lake District that I think of now when I hear, 'The heavens are telling the glory of God', from Haydn's 'Creation'. We did have a minor problem with one of the minibuses. I was in the second one, driven by Richard Grant, when we entered the lakeside car park at Keswick. As we followed the others, who were already in the car park, we heard a metallic shrieking noise and registered it was our roof rack parting company with the van as we passed under the bar to restrict tall vehicles from entering. With several engineers in the group we managed to reattach the roof rack for the return journey but we did not get all our deposit back when we returned the vehicles to Marshall's in Cambridge.

The Easter term brought exams and I got more and more anxious about them as term progressed. For revision I got hold of some old Part IA papers. Most people seemed to just read lecture notes but I had always worked to understand lectures as I went along. It is easy to read maths and think you understand it but it is only by trying to solve problems that you really learn. Unlike at school, there was help for questions I could not do but I slowly became able to look at the papers with the expectation that I might be able to find something that I could answer. My brother was, at the same time, studying for maths finals at Bristol University, although he had already taken half his exams, immediately after the Easter vacation. Not long before my first exam I got a message from the college porters to call home. My brother had been taken ill with a kidney infection and had been sent home in a very stressed and agitated state. I continued work and tried not to worry about him.

Last minute revision has never appealed to me because I find it counterproductive. It just increases my anxiety. I was not the only one to feel like this and Andrew Ellis, Mike Farthing, David Wilson and myself did something about it. We started a tradition that the day before exams we would get out the Jacques croquet set from the sports pavilion and take out our frustration on each others balls as we roqueted our way around the college croquet lawn, which was just below the tennis courts, probably where Cowan Court is now. I could never get the set out myself as it lived in the gents changing rooms!

The first-year exams were held on the spring bank holiday Monday and Tuesday at the graduate centre next to the Garden

House Hotel, which was being rebuilt after a fire. The building work was disturbing and I quickly got a headache. I did feel calmer as I started work on the first of the four three hour papers that we sat on two consecutive days. The tourists outside, sunbathing and punting by the mill pond, seemed to be a world away. We sat alphabetically in exams and for three years I sat immediately behind Richard Pinch, from Trinity, feeling intimidated by his confidence. By the end of the two days I was exhausted and convinced myself the exams were a disaster, as I focused on the mistakes I had made.

Meanwhile, Bristol University had arranged for my brother to sit the second half of his finals at Swansea University. He had to sit the exams in order to avoid receiving an aegrotat, an unclassified degree, even though he was not really fit enough. Nevertheless Bristol University awarded him a first class degree and, although a job awaited him at the Post Office Telecommunications, he decided he wanted to do a Ph.D. in stochastic processes. He asked for my help. I approached Geoff Eagleson, a statistics fellow at Churchill, and my father brought David with him when he came to pick me up at the end of my first year, so that he could be interviewed for a Ph.D. place. The results of the first-year exams had not yet been released, but as my father, David and myself squeezed into Geoff Eagleson's VW beetle for a visit to the Stats lab, he congratulated me on how well I had done. I had not realised he was one of the Part IA examiners that year so had inside knowledge. After we had returned to Swansea for the summer I heard that I had obtained first class marks and was awarded a scholarship, not only for the coming year but also retrospectively for the previous year. I had not registered that the women in the newly mixed colleges were not eligible for entrance scholarships. The women's colleges would not agree to it, as they feared that it would mean they would lose the best women. I can only see this as discrimination against women by women. At Churchill, both women and men, who were not already scholars, were awarded retrospective scholarships if their exam marks warranted it. The names of Cambridge scholars were published in *The Times* newspaper to my embarrassment and my mother's pleasure.

David was still not entirely well so although I had planned to work over the summer my parents required me to spend my time with David. He was prescribed the minor tranquilliser, Valium, which was a new drug, marketed as non-addictive. I learnt to be suspicious of marketing promises as Valium is very addictive and, inconsequentially, blu tack does take paint off walls. David and I had a good time together that summer and we moved beyond our days of childhood bickering. I read the novels that I had bought during the year. We wandered around Swansea, playing golf at the nine-hole links, where the hazards of the bunkers were added to by the road on one side and the sea on the other. We went up to London together to the Proms at Royal Albert Hall, staying with our grandfather in Southend, and visited art galleries and museums during the day. We must have looked comfortable together because, more than once, the photographers who touted around the Tower of London tried to get us to pose for photos, as if we were boyfriend and girlfriend, as we rushed to not miss the Southend train from Fenchurch Street Station. We even went on a mystery train trip from Swansea when we had no idea of the destination. As we skirted the north of London, we had a sudden premonition where we were going and discovered that it is possible to get to Southend and back in a day, with enough time to visit the funfair and go to the end of the mile and a quarter long pier. Southend-on-Mud would have seemed a more honest name than Southend-on-Sea and it was not the destination we were hoping for, as we were already familiar enough with the mud flats of the Thames estuary. At the end of the summer we went with my schoolfriend, Liz Jones, to Killarney in Eire where we learnt why Ireland is so green. There was torrential rain and low cloud for a week but it did save me from walking in Macgillycuddy's reeks and climbing Carrauntoohil, the highest peak in Ireland. Instead we enjoyed the Irish mist.

Part IA

In theory the vacations were the time to get finances back on track. With no summer job I was unable to save any money that first summer. I was fortunate, compared with many other students, that my parents did pay their full contribution to the means-tested grant and gave me some extra for spending time with David. In 1972 a full grant was £480 at Cambridge, Oxford and London and £420 elsewhere. The following year it went up to £520 at all universities except for London, recognising that there was no good reason for Oxbridge students to receive more. In those days it was possible to go to university from any background and not get into debt, as long as you did not smoke, drink or eat out to excess. Inflation was rampant in the seventies but debt was much less of a problem. Credit cards did not exist and there were very few ways in which money could be borrowed. I graduated without debt. I was lucky.

So that brings me to the end of my first year at Cambridge. As I write I find more and more memories returning. I spent some time thinking about whether I should name people. As you can tell I have mostly decided to use names. I hope they are accurate. Some names I simply do not remember. Others may have got confused in my mind. It is not my intention to offend anyone. I have heard it said that everyone who knows the author gets offended by their autobiography. Upset is caused both by excluding people who might have been included and by including people who do not like what is said about them. I have tried to say positive things about those I name but may not have not always succeeded. However this is my story. It is my life as I remember it.

My instinct in writing something that is about the past is to want to use other people's records and to check the accuracy of everything I have written. Twenty five years ago, as a student of theology, including church history, I was always complimented on staying attached to primary sources. Then I was mostly writing about the far distant past, where I have no experience of my own to bring. My own life is something that I know better than anything I could read in a book. My memory may not be completely reliable but I bring something that cannot be found in other records. I know what it was like at the time. I was there. In writing now I am coming to more appreciate the historical novel as a literary genre. Imagination can bring to life things that are otherwise just a dry record of what was thought to be important at the time. The past can be recorded with a view to changing reality, not to accurately reporting it. It is a cliché to say that history is written by the winners but it is always written from a particular viewpoint. There is no such thing as objective history, just as in quantum mechanics observing a system changes it.

3. Part IB

I arrived at college for my second year feeling much more settled. College felt like home, especially as my brother had now followed me to Churchill to start a Ph.D. on stochastic modelling with Peter Whittle, a college fellow and university professor. David no longer had to feel jealous of his little sister and we grew into friends. Richard Grant had graduated and stayed on for a Ph.D. in engineering so I found myself with postgraduate, as well as undergraduate friends. I knew I could hold my own academically and no longer felt intimidated by my peers.

The year began with a trip up to London to visit the electrical discount stores that lined Tottenham Court Road, north of Oxford Street, in the 1970s. I had my scholarship money of £120 and, to my mother's disgust, spent £80 on a record deck, amplifier and speakers. I had asked around, worked my way through a number of hi-fi magazines, and decided to buy the Garrard SP25 Mk 3 record deck, a best seller of its era, along with a Rotel amplifier and floor standing speakers, with large woofers, that were just about big enough to function as side tables. I was glad my brother came with me to help manhandle my new property on and off the train and into a taxi back to Churchill. It looked and sounded good set up on my window seat.

My new room, 44H, was a little larger and overlooked a modern sculpture of three figures, which I initially thought was by Henry Moore, but later discovered was by Sean Crampton, a lesser known sculptor. I acquired a new poster of a classic painting by Brueghel of children's games. Above me, in room 44P, was a first year engineer, Judy Roberts, who liked loud music. Fortunately she was out most of the day but I did have to learn to put up with my ceiling resonating with the bass notes of her favourite bands. I could now compete and played Gershwin's 'Rhapsody in Blue' in retaliation. I favoured classical music and slowly gathered a collection of Bach, Beethoven, Debussy, Dvorak, Rachmaninov and Sibelius. David bought me records of Smetana's 'Ma Vlast' to thank me for agreeing to spend the previous summer with him, even though I had been given no choice. Vltava became a favourite and many years later, on a trip from Berlin to Prague we drove along the banks of the river into Prague. I joined in lustily as Lord Leslie Griffiths, who happened to have booked the same holiday as us, encouraged those in the coach to hum the tune along with him. In my second year, as I worked in my room I drank endless mugs of filter coffee and was accompanied by the strains of classical music, and the smells from burning candles and joss sticks. When my mother visited my room, she informed me, in no uncertain terms, that people only burnt joss sticks to cover up the smell of drugs and I should stop it as once, which encouraged me to burn more. The perfumes of sandalwood and jasmine seemed to inspire me.

During term-time I did not watch television, except for the obligatory viewing of Doctor Who. This was so popular that if you wanted a seat in the Junior Common Room, where the only set was located, you had to watch the preceding program, 'Jim'll Fix It'. I would not be surprised if that program is written out of history. It will certainly not be repeated endlessly as it has fallen from grace like its presenter, Jimmy Saville, with his massive cigars. I had been watching Doctor Who since its first episode in 1963 when I would have hidden behind the sofa if we had had one. The prospect of daleks in the London underground can still raise the hairs on the back of my neck.

Chapel life changed in my second year with the arrival of Richard Cain, the new college chaplain. Richard had previously been chaplain at the University of Warwick and came with his wife, Judith, and their four young children. Noel Duckworth had lived in college but a house was found for Richard and his family in Storeys Way. I continued to go to the evening services and I think there was no longer a morning service. The evening preachers became quite eclectic. There were the worthy ones who wanted to ensure we were theologically well educated. There were others who reminded us that Jesus's disciples were not educated. Richard became friends with John Robinson, dean of Trinity College and author of *Honest to God*, who had a liberal perspective. I appreciated John Taylor, Bishop of Winchester, who understood that we did not need intellectual input and read us the story of the velveteen rabbit who became real because he was loved. About once a month the service was followed by a meal and discussion, often at Richard's home. On one of those occasions the speaker was a lady from Brixton who worked with the community and had to cope with addicts and sometimes stabbings. She spoke of a world I did not know and I am sure that listening to her provided a better education than any doctrinal theology would.

At that time there was a chapel committee, made up of the chaplain and some of the regular attenders at services; while the college trustees met separately. I became chapel treasurer, for one year, and had my first adventures with double entry bookkeeping. Fortunately there were never many transactions. I had to pay the small change from collections into the bank, pay the college for our electricity usage and pay the expenses of visiting preachers. I was often amused at the responses that I got to the cheques I had sent, usually addressed to Revd. J.Y. Probert. Perhaps they knew something that I did not. Our income and expenditure generally matched; at least they did until someone managed to send a golf ball through one of the Piper stained glass windows. The repair was going to cost about £500, equal to our entire annual expenditure. I cannot recall how it was paid in the end. I think the bill went to the trustees but it did result in mesh being put up outside the windows so the same thing could not happen again. At the committee meetings we talked about forthcoming services and dealt with problems. The chaplain was keen to allow a group of Sufi dancers to use the chapel; Sufi dancers being the whirling dervishes of the Muslim world. This caused a problem with the chapel trustees as the trust deed only allowed the chapel to be used for Christian activities. I think this was the beginning of difficulties between Richard Cain and the trustees.

The course that I was taking at Cambridge is known as the maths tripos. Divided into three parts like a three legged stool, a Bachelor of Arts degree is awarded on completion of Part II. Almost all students took Part I over two years so in my second year I was studying Part IB maths. There had been no choice of courses in the first year but in the second year we could start to specialise and I favoured the applied side choosing mechanics of elastic media, electro-magnetic theory and fluid dynamics over group theory and topology. I liked being able to see the applications of what we were studying. The fluids course was taught by George Batchelor, author of the textbook we used, and I became adept at calculating flow around spheres and aerofoils. It was handy that exactly the same mathematical techniques could be used for electro-magnetic theory. Dr Ralph Lapwood taught the mechanics of elastic media and he had a very gentle and clear style of lecturing. He had worked in China until 1952 and remained passionate in his love of that country and its people. I found him quite endearing as he referred to all male students by their surnames and added a title to the women, so by the time he retired in 1976 he was calling me Miss Probert. I did come to a realisation over the year as to why I was less attracted to pure maths, which is usually presented as definitions which are then used to prove theorems. It is presented as something incontrovertible, factual and coldly logical. There is no discussion as to where the definitions come from. Some of my friends were now studying mathematical logic. I learnt that Russell and Whitehead had tried to systematise the whole of mathematics in their tome, *Principia Mathematica*, starting from set theory. They thought it true that any mathematical statement could be proved either true or false. A few years later Kurt Gödel proved that every formal system is either incomplete, inconsistent or inadequate and Russell and Whitehead's optimism was unfounded. I realised now that definitions are chosen so that theorems are true; the opposite of the way that maths is taught. Knowing that helped me appreciate pure mathematics more as I could now see its true creativity. In some sense, the problem at the heart of mathematics is the inability to be able to prove that anything exists. René Descartes, in the seventeenth century, thought he had proved our existence with the statement, 'I think, therefore I am.' Proving that the 'I' connected with a thought is the same 'I' connected with subsequent thoughts is impossible. It is generally a good idea in everyday life to assume that people and things do exist, but, in a formal sense, it is as hard to prove that 'I' exist as it is to prove that 'God' exists. I did not move into formal study of mathematical logic, as it is not an area with good employment prospects, but it remains an area that intrigues me. I have now studied some philosophy as part of a theology degree and am left with the thought that we are not as enlightened as we sometimes imagine.

So, back to reality. Inflation was rampant. Oil prices were at an all time high. To restrict petrol consumption a nationwide maximum speed limit of 50 miles per hour was introduced. The 70 miles per hour speed limit had been introduced by Barbara Castle on safety grounds in 1966, prior to which there had been no maximum speed limit on many roads. I recall people trying to see if their cars would run at the maximum speed the manufacturers promised. With the high inflation wages were falling behind prices. The unions became more militant and in late 1973 80% of miners voted to strike from the beginning of 1974. Most power stations were oil or coal-powered and in order to preserve supplies the prime minister, Edward Heath, moved the country to a three day week, where industries could choose which three days to work but could not extend their hours beyond their normal hours. Television stopped broadcasting at 10.30pm and pubs closed early to reduce power consumption at night. These measures did not impinge much on the students at college where we had neither cars nor televisions. There were long power cuts. My candles were used to provide light and we used to sit and talk during the blackouts. I was scared that the world would end, which now seems to me rather melodramatic. I was reminded of the essay I had written for the Use of English exam when the end of the world came when all the lights went out. Edward Heath called a general election in February 1974 and the result was a hung parliament. This led to a minority labour government with Harold Wilson becoming prime minister. The miners' strike ended on 6th March when an offer of a 35% pay rise was accepted. The three day week ended and a second general election in October 1974 resulted in a small labour majority. The world had not ended.

By Easter 1974 things were a bit more stable. I had got involved with supporting international students through Mark Ruston, vicar of the Round Church, and returned to the Lake District for an Easter holiday with a number of these students plus some members of CICCU, the Cambridge Christian Union. I think four of us went from Churchill C.U; myself, my brother, Jackie Mehra and Michael You, a first year mathematician from Singapore. We stayed in a large house near Ullswater where we could again admire the daffodils fluttering and dancing in the breeze. Of the international students the largest group was Iranian women studying English at a language school in Cambridge. They were very westernised but were not used to British country life. They were hoping for more shopping and less hiking but they did enjoy it when snow fell. We found wellington boots to replace their smart footwear and introduced them to snowmen and snowball fights. I wonder now what happened to those women after the overthrow of the Shah of Iran in 1979. They would not have been supporters of Ayatollah Khomeini.

Part IB

As a scholar I received two invitations from the Master and Fellows of Churchill College to formal meals; one was the Founders Feast to which all undergraduates were invited and the other a meal just for scholars. The required attire for these meals was black tie and gown, although I had more than a suspicion that it would have been frowned upon if I had turned up dressed in just a black tie and gown, how ever many safety pins I used on the front of the gown to keep myself decent! Over the summer I had made myself two long dresses for these and other social occasions. One was in a floral red material with plenty of frills and a 1960s hippy feel to it. The other was a little more sophisticated but did look better with a gown over the top. It was made of a pink brushed cotton fabric to which I had added a brown embroidered ribbon on the bodice, cuffs and hems. It was while wearing this homage to Churchill College at one of the formal meals that I learnt from one of the fellows the history of the pink and chocolate brown college colours. Apparently, at an early meeting of the founder trustees, when Winston Churchill was present, there was a discussion about what to choose as the new college colours. It had to be something different from any existing college but there was a desire that they should look good too. As the discussion heated up, Sir Winston interjected, suggesting that the college could use his racing colours. This brought the discussion to a close as this was accepted by one and all as an excellent idea. It was only on leaving that most of the fellows learnt what they had agreed to. I have not checked the veracity of this story but think it more likely to be true than a currently circulating story that pink and chocolate were the colours of Clementine Churchill's favourite ice-cream.

The formal meals now proceeded almost without incident. I would borrow an undergraduate gown, often from David Race, one of the C.U. mathematicians, and hope that nothing was dropped onto it. I only once had an incident with Stilton cheese and the gown, which did require a bit of dry cleaning and a scented spray. I was by now adept with sherry, followed by white wine and then red wine, but had not quite got worked out what to do with the port and claret. At the first Scholars' Feast I attended there were two separate seating plans. During the main course I recall an interesting conversation with one of the trustees of the Tate gallery who was present as a guest. We changed seats for dessert and I found myself at the end of high table seated near an economics fellow and his guest, who was drinking steadily. He seemed somewhat lecherous as he poured port for me and, noticing the name on my place marker, recalled that there was also a Probert in Dylan Thomas' *Under Milk Wood*. I was very lucky that he was offended when I replied that the person he was thinking of was Rosie Probert, the local prostitute, whose line was 'Come on up, boys.' I guess he realised that I was not about to succumb to his 'charm' and I made it back to my room alone at the end of the meal. This was the only time during the nine years I spent in Cambridge that I felt at risk from a sexual predator. Drunkards can be obnoxious anywhere. I did spend the night dreaming that I was at sea on a ship in rough seas and awoke with a splitting headache. I did not know then that I had been drinking port from the larger claret glass. The hangover did put me off drinking port for a year or two, after which I discovered a small glass with a little Stilton provides a pleasant end to a rich meal.

There were times when too much alcohol flowed freely. Rooms were allocated by a ballot and friends would try to get rooms near each other. This meant some staircases were rowdier than others and staircase parties were the rowdiest events. I avoided them, because I did not enjoy loud music, dancing or getting drunk. Fortunately my friends felt the same way so we would move to quieter parts of college when there was a party on. This meant I was not there to witness one of the mathematicians in our year leaning backwards while resting on a second floor window seat and falling onto the grass bordering Storey's Way. Apparently he walked back into college past the porters in the lodge and put himself to bed. In the morning he could not move because he had broken his pelvis. He was put in plaster and out of action for some time but his experience provided strong evidence that alcohol numbs pain. I decided it was worth refraining from getting drunk.

Terms at Cambridge have always seemed to me to be strangely named. Starting with the Michaelmas term in the autumn, Lent term follows in the spring with Easter term running until June, when the May balls take place. Sometimes I found myself worrying that the exams would be before Easter and not after. At least I did not have to refer to Hilary and Trinity terms, as the spring and summer terms are called at Oxford. Cambridge may be odd but not quite as odd as some other places. By April and May supervisions were concentrating on revision. In my second year the work was helped along by Ann Dowling who supervised Churchill students for Fluids I. She was a Ph.D. student in engineering from Girton College, but was married to Tom Hynes, a Ph.D. student from Churchill, and they lived in the Wolfson flats up the road from the main college buildings, near the chapel. It did not occur to me then that I would spend three years living in the same flats. Some of my anxiety was allayed by answering old exam questions and getting help when I was stuck but I was still very afraid that I might fail and be thrown out of college.

Our second year exams consisted of six three hour papers over three days, starting on the spring bank holiday. By the end we were all exhausted and celebrated by going to see the 1968 Stanley Kubrick film 2001: A Space Odyssey at the Arts Cinema. Before term ended a group of twelve of us, largely from our Mah Jongg group, went on a midnight punting expedition down to Grantchester. We used two punts belonging to other colleges which had been arranged by Ian Grayson, a third year chemist and boyfriend of Alison Rudd. Twelve of us set off at about midnight, after a meal. The group included someone from Newnham and a geologist from Queens, who had acquired the punts. We made it down to Grantchester and I mostly remember how cold it was. I did not object to snuggling under a blanket with the geologist from Queens as he kept me warm but I did decline his suggestion that I should return to his room. I guessed that he had more than breakfast in mind. Returning to college well after dawn, I do recall feeling very groggy later that morning at a meeting to talk about third year courses.

That summer I had my first paid job working at the nuclear research labs at Berkeley on the banks of the River Severn. The previous summer I had received a letter from college not only telling me that I was to become a scholar but also suggesting that any man with a scholarship could apply for an additional scholarship from the CEGB (Central Electricity Generating Board). Not being a man I had not applied but I had discovered on returning to college after the summer that there had been no intention to exclude women. This led to me applying to work with the CEGB in the vacation, and, following an interview when I had to describe how a nuclear power station worked, I was given a summer placement. I was put with a group testing the design for pressure vessels using novel finite element methods, sharing an office with two permanent members of staff, one of whom was my boss. I spent most of the summer working on a cylindrically symmetric mesh designed to fit the shape of the steam generating heavy water reactor and running programs to carry out a stress analysis of the vessel. The Berkeley nuclear labs ran safety tests on reactors designed elsewhere, usually on equipment that the government had already rejected as too expensive. It was an extremely male working environment, which caused me no problems, except in one long corridor with many sets of doors. Somewhere near the beginning of the corridor, a door would usually be opened for me, then I was in front and found myself having to open all the rest of the doors for everyone else. After a while I took to hanging back. We called each other by first names which seemed friendly to me even though most of the staff were two or three times my age. My mother thought this was entirely wrong and that I should address my elders (and hence necessarily betters) as Mr Darleston, or Dr Price as appropriate. I think it was just that times were changing.

I stayed in digs in Dursley on the edge of the Cotswolds and used a CEGB-provided coach to get to work. I was paid weekly with a brown paper envelope containing just over seventeen pounds. It seemed reasonable pay to me, although if I had obtained the CEGB scholarship I would have received thirty pounds. My digs cost ten pounds a week or a bit less if I was away at the weekend, so I did not save a lot of money. I liked the area and enjoyed the weekends, walking up to the Stinchcombe Hill golf course and across the hills to Stroud. I did not attend church anywhere that summer but walked instead. The churches in the town all looked too Victorian and staid for me to want to enter. On one occasion I visited the Tyndale Monument at North Nibley, collecting the key from the local pub and returning it afterwards, so I could reflect on the life of William Tyndale who had wanted the bible to be understood by every ploughboy. These were the illiterate people of the time. I did not know then that Churchill College had been built on old ploughed fields but I once met a monk at Turvey Abbey, near Bedford, who had worked on them as a young man. He was pleased to meet someone who studied on the land that he had ploughed.

4. Part II

Returning to Churchill in October 1974 for my third year, I acquired two new posters; one of the Escher waterfall that appears to run uphill and the other a black and white painting by Bridget Riley with lines so close and twisty that they looked as if they were moving. They provided an interesting contrast to my poster of Brueghel's sixteenth century painting. I moved to room 44P so had a higher outlook. Beneath me, Alison Rudd moved into my old room.

As the third year started I began to think about what I wanted to do on graduation and realised I wanted to do more maths. I was pleased that I had again obtained first class marks in the exams and remained a scholar, which meant that I had reasonable prospects of being able to stay on for Part III maths and a Ph.D. was a real possibility. This removed some pressure from me and meant that I did not need to take time off for interviews. I continued studying applied maths, adding some courses in quantum mechanics. Just for fun, I attended most of John Conway's graph theory course. His lectures were always inspiring. He had the ability to present difficult material and make it seem simple, although even he could not give a simple proof to the four colour theorem, which was at that time an unproven conjecture. When the proof came in 1976, Appel and Haken first used some manipulation to make the problem finite, then used a computer to finally prove that no more than four colours are ever needed to colour different areas on a flat map. Mathematicians always look for beautiful proofs but sometimes truth is not elegant. Quantum mechanics was taught by John Polkinghorne, who later became a full-time Anglican priest. His style was precise and clear, although somewhat dry. He had a habit of flicking chalk at students who were talking in his lectures. I have a fantasy of him doing the same thing from church pulpits but he must have given up the habit. In 2002 he won the Templeton Prize, which honours a living person who has made an exceptional contribution to affirming life's spiritual dimension whether through insight, discovery, or practical works. I met him again at a number of talks, most memorably when he was speaking of Christianity in an extra-terrestrial world of little green men. Keith Moffatt taught Fluids II and I admired his pure Scottish accent. Supervisions were held in college where we still worked our way through endless example sheets. Andy Cliffe, my supervision partner, and myself could mostly solve these problems without help so supervisions with Douglas Gough, a college fellow and astrophysicist, moved onto areas not covered in lectures. He talked to us about convection in the sun and the similarities between the sun and a cup of tea, in terms of the angular momentum gained in stirring tea. Ali Alpar, a Ph.D. student in particle physics, gave us supervisions in quantum physics in his college room. Coming from Ankara, he educated us not only in particle spin but also in Turkish etiquette. The ritual of the supervision included boiling up sweet, thick coffee in a copper pot on the calor gas stove that he kept on his sarcophagus. It would clearly have been an insult not to drink it. If you are wondering how a sarcophagus came to be in a college room, it was simply a feature. The window seats in most rooms housed the heating pipes and a fan to circulate hot air. If there was no window seat, these were placed across the room inside a large cuboidal granite plinth, which also acted as a room divider; known as sarcophagi, they were never used, as far as I know, to conceal bodies, although that was their function in antiquity. Andy preferred the Turkish coffee that Ali served to anything I ever offered him, especially Earl Grey tea, which he despised, complaining it tasted of after shave lotion, which I cannot imagine he ever actually drank.

I guess that I spent quite a lot of time with Andy in my third year. He was engaged to be married and was actively looking for a job. To his relief, he eventually secured a position at the research labs at Harwell which was the start of a successful career. He could easily have stayed on for a Ph.D. but enjoyed the working environment at Harwell, where he was involved in basic fluid dynamics research. When commercial pressures meant that it was no longer possible to engage in pure research, he succeeded in getting a chair at the University of Loughborough, so became one of an elite group of professors without a doctorate. After graduation, we met from time to time at conferences and, after I left maths, we kept some contact through Dave Lever who also spent his career at Harwell. It was with sadness that I learnt Andy Cliffe had contracted cancer and died in 2014.

A major surprise came in my life when one of my friends wanted a deeper relationship. I was used to having more male friends than female; something which remains the case. It does not seem unusual to me and I still find all female environments more intimidating than primarily male ones. However, one evening, sitting drinking coffee and chatting in the room of Andrew Ellis, I realised that an arm was not just resting on my shoulders but holding me affectionately. Next to me was Ian Holyer, who seemed as surprised at his action as I was. I was not sure how to respond but it was definitely something that I welcomed. I had not noticed he might have been interested in me but I have a feeling that Andrew Ellis had guessed and was trying to help us to get together. Ian and I started to meet before dinner and spent many evenings together, often playing records. We were both fans of Flanders and Swann, probably best known for their 'Hippopotamus Song'. I owned the records to 'At the Drop of a Hat' and 'At the Drop of Another Hat' and Ian owned 'The Bestiary'. We used to joke that we had to get together to amalgamate our record collections. We still played Mah Jongg, went to bible study groups and met in larger groups as well as spending time together on our own. One evening I decided it was time to cook a meal for Ian, with a view to impressing him. This was a new venture for me and I had to buy a saucepan, as well as the necessary ingredients for the pork and rice recipe that I had found in a magazine. This included buying a clove of garlic. I had not previously prepared garlic. I think the rest is predictable. I wondered why such a fuss was made about crushing garlic cloves. We ate the meal, including what I now know was a bulb of garlic, and the smell lingered on the staircase for weeks. It must have been love, for Ian was not discouraged. In February 1975, Ian's parents came to college to take him out for his 21st birthday. I did meet them but we did not mention why I was hanging around, so they went off to lunch at the Italian restaurant in the market square, while I stayed in college and had the usual cafeteria lunch, with no garlic.

Students were encouraged to play a part in the life of the chapel and sometimes one of us was asked to preach. This led to my first sermon. I had taken part in various Sunday School activities as a child but this was new and scary. I borrowed the idea for my sermon from Peter Marshall, a former Chaplain of the United States Senate, whose biography, *A Man Called Peter*, was popular in C.U. circles. I do not recall what biblical text I was using but it might have been, 'Let us *run* with perseverance the race marked out for us, fixing our eyes on Jesus, the pioneer and perfecter of faith.' Using the triangular warning sign for falling or fallen rocks as an illustration, I pointed out that we have to continue on the road of life set before us and pay attention to our surroundings. We do not turn back because we can see trouble ahead but may, wisely, look out for rocks to avoid on the road. I do not think it was a great sermon but it did help me work out how to use notes for public speaking. By using short lines and indents, I found I could easily keep my eye on what I needed to say next, while still appearing to be looking at those who were listening. It worked so well that when either lecturing or preaching later I was often complimented on not using notes, when actually I was reading my notes almost verbatim.

The varied services at chapel continued to inspire me. There were two excellent organists in Halvard White and Diarmaid MacCulloch, a Ph.D. student in Reformation church history. Diarmaid ran a choir and I enjoyed listening to him singing falsetto, in harmony with the other members. Each year, at Pentecost, a joint mass was held, with the Anglican priest, Richard Cain, concelebrating with a Roman Catholic priest, Joe Ching, a Jesuit from St Edmund's House. We would have a picnic afterwards on the playing fields and fly kites, as is appropriate on a day that marks the wind of the spirit descending on the church. An invitation to eat at St Edmund's House took me to another new Cambridge environment. St Edmund's was established after the repeal of the Test Act in 1871 to enable Roman Catholic men to attend the university and its atmosphere seemed almost medieval. Instead of water there was ale to drink on the tables; old-fashioned weak ale that was probably first offered in the days of cholera when water was not safe to drink. I registered how much Catholics and other non-conformists have in common. Although many people think of Methodists as teetotal, before the nineteenth century it was a requirement that ale was provided for church meetings. John Wesley strongly disapproved of tea drinking, as people were impoverishing themselves to buy it. On our holiday from Berlin to Prague, one morning I had joined Lord Leslie Griffiths, minister at Wesley's Chapel, London, at breakfast and we both noticed the champagne and smoked salmon available. As we drank I asked him, tongue-in-cheek, how much he would pay me not tell his congregation that he enjoyed champagne for breakfast. He said he would be proud for his congregation to know and that he was just following in the footsteps of John Wesley who, every year, ordered a dozen cases of claret to see him through the cold Bristol winter.

Not many of the Churchill fellows regularly came to chapel and those who did were mostly chapel trustees. Richard Hey, a geologist, was a frequent attender and something of a father figure to us as undergraduates. He was an opera fan, which we only discovered after we had moved to Bristol and found him in the audience of performances of the Welsh National Opera at the Hippodrome. Captain Roskill sometimes came to chapel but much preferred services from the Book of Common Prayer to the more modern, up-to-date and relevant services of Richard Cain. Hywel George, the college bursar, was a Welsh non-conformist from the same sort of background as myself and he possessed an accent just like my father's. He was less enamoured with traditional worship and fully supported the interdenominational nature of chapel. The radio astronomer, Tony Hewish, was a more intermittent attender at chapel but when we asked him he willingly came to talk to the college C.U. about faith.

Awarded the Nobel Prize in late 1974 with Martin Ryle for the discovery of pulsars, Tony Hewish held a formal dinner early the following year for the scholars of the college to celebrate, at which his gold medal was passed around from hand to hand with a view to inspiring us. It will remain the closest I ever get to a Nobel Prize. There was controversy at the time that his research student, Jocelyn Bell, had not also been named as a prize winner. When Tony Hewish spoke at that dinner in 1975 he was clear that without her work there would have been no discovery and that she should also have received the prize. He was unequivocal. I was very disappointed some years later when I heard him talking on TV about the discovery and he claimed that it was a project he had set up and anyone working for him would have made the discovery. What Jocelyn did was akin to finding a needle in a haystack. It would be laughable if the farmer who had designed the haystack claimed he had found the needle. Very few women have ever won the Nobel prize in science subjects and the nomination process does seem to work against equality. Fortunately, the omission did not seem to damage the career of

Dame Jocelyn Bell Burnell and she is probably more well-known now than Tony Hewish.

At the next formal meal I was to attend I discovered I was to be seated at high table to the right of the Master, Sir William Hawthorne, known as Bill to the undergraduates. I was very surprised to be allocated this apparent seat of honour. The left hand side has higher precedence and is the direction in which the meal is served and in which the port rotates, but I discovered that if the Master is talking to the person to their right then they are served immediately after the Master. I enjoyed the conversation. I knew the Master was an engineer interested in fluids and had worked with Frank Whittle during WWII on jet engines. I talked about the fluids courses I was taking and he told me about the rubber devices, called Dracones, that he had designed during the Suez crisis to transport oil in the Mediterranean and drew a picture of one on a serviette. I misheard him at the time and thought he had designed dragoons in WWII. In those days it was hard to check up on information and it was on googling recently that I was amused to find my error. I was glad I did not know at the time that he had not been in favour of the college going mixed. I had also not known before the dinner that my tutor, John Knott, was responsible for the seating plans for formal meals. It was encouraging to discover that John thought I was a positive advert for the college having gone mixed. I always found William Hawthorne very gracious. In my first year he and his wife had invited all the students around in small groups to the Master's lodge for afternoon tea. I felt very welcome there, not least because the lodge had exactly the same white, shaggy-piled carpet that my parents had in their living room in Swansea. I would never have guessed he had not wanted female students. I hope he had changed his mind.

My brother and I were still working with international students. One of them was a Vietnamese refugee who had settled in the UK. He was older than me but studying for A-levels. He frequently came around to my room in college looking for help. I did wonder if he was looking for more but felt completely secure now that I was in a relationship of my own. In the 1970s Tyndale House, in Selwyn Gardens, near Newnham College, was often used for social gatherings. It was there that I first noticed my brother behaving out of character with a student from Newnham College. He started inviting her to college. Penelope Horsburgh was in the early stages of an engineering Ph.D., studying the properties of transistors. She lived in digs on Madingley Road just opposite Churchill, in the attic room of Stanley Booth Clibborn, the vicar of Great Saint Mary's University Church and later Bishop of Manchester. I would have found it an intimidating place to live fearing my behaviour was not good enough but it seemed to suit Penny. As 1974 moved in to 1975 it was clear to David and I that we were both in serious relationships. This meant it was in the interests of both of us not to divulge any secrets to my parents. David had a phone in the set he was sharing with an American postgrad. He regularly received calls from home enquiring about what we were up to. I was regularly complained at for not keeping in touch but I had to queue up if I wanted to use one of the phones that were just outside the library in the centre of college. This meant that my mother did not know anything about my growing friendship, although she did know about Penny, to whom David became engaged in early 1975. She warmly approved of Penny, who was the daughter of a headmistress and a deputy headmaster. She judged people by their parentage. I always liked the idea that Penny might have got together with my friend Mike Farthing, making her a Penny Farthing, but it was not to be. Love seems to be quite idiosyncratic.

By Easter 1975 things were getting serious between myself and Ian, to the extent that I risked inviting him to stay for a week in Swansea. I had never before invited anyone to stay. This was the last vacation before our finals but our minds were not on academic matters. On Good Friday 1975 we embarked on a boat trip across the Bristol Channel aboard the MV Balmoral, a Campbell's steamer, that made regular summer trips for tourists from Swansea docks across to the Devon coast. Now, at its winter berth in the centre of Bristol, I see the Balmoral most days, reminding of a time when we were both younger and in a better state of repair. Easter came early in 1975 and on the 28th March the weather was extremely variable. We arrived at the Victorian seaside resort of Ilfracombe in sunshine. Walking around the harbour we stopped at a bench to admire the view, or so I thought. Ian had something else in mind and it was there that he asked if I would marry him. I entered a state of shock but managed to stammer a yes. I felt then that this relationship was something God-given and we prayed on that bench, thanking God and asking for God's blessing on our future together. As the weather deteriorated we left the bench and sheltered from the rain in a cheap restaurant near the waterfront, where we ate lunch and had a celebratory drink. The rain turned to snow and we watched children tobogganing down Capstone hill. We discussed engagement rings and decided to shop for one together in Cambridge. Lingering over lunch, the snow began to give way to sunshine and we wandered back to the ship along Capstone Parade, buying Ian a trendy tie at The Smugglers craft shop on the way. That tie seems very dated now; a narrow belt of rough spun brown material with a green, mossy strip up the middle, which we started to call his country lane tie. It was my present to Ian and I am not sure Ian ever appreciated it as much as me but he wore it to please me. As we returned to Swansea, on the swell of the Bristol Channel, the sunshine again gave way to sleety showers. I have seldom felt so cold but it provided a good excuse to cuddle up to Ian. When we arrived home I was told my schoolfriend, Liz Jones, had visited; coming to the front door with her horse. She was informed I had a friend staying and we had gone out for the day but 'there was nothing in it'.

Hence it was a surprise when we announced that we had got engaged. My mother's initial reaction was that I must be pregnant and her second reaction was that I was just copying my brother. She did not credit me with any common sense. A phone call to

Cambridge established my brother's support for me, as he said it was obvious we were about to get engaged. Ian had been brought up Roman Catholic, which caused concern. 'How will we tell Auntie Edwina?' my mother enquired. This was my father's aunt in Pontypridd, who was the daughter of a Baptist minister. She was very happy when we told her. It was my mother who was prejudiced. Eventually the Christmas bottle of cherry brandy was opened and my mother capitulated, while my father sat by quietly pleased. Ian returned to his parent's home in Northamptonshire for the rest of the Easter vac. Ian's dad picked him up from the station and was not very surprised to hear that Ian had got engaged. He trusted Ian's judgement. Ian's parents were both Roman Catholic converts; his father from atheism and his mother from the Anglo-Catholic wing of the Anglican church. They had no problem at all with my faith. I always felt at home with Ian's family. Ian had joined the Navigators at college, rather than the Christian Union, and had spent two years on their discipleship courses which had a detrimental effect on his academic work. He had left the Navigators before we got together, moving to the more tolerant Churchill C.U., where Catholics were welcome. Ian was now coming with me to the Round Church and we continued to go to college chapel. Neither he nor his parents had any desire for me to become a Roman Catholic. They were clear that faith and freedom must go together. When the Easter term began Ian presented me with a marquetry picture of Herstmonceux castle, which was then the home of the Royal Greenwich Observatory. I was glad he had missed me.

We bought a solitaire diamond engagement ring at Ratner's for £50. It seemed to me like a lot of money but it was expected at the time. Whenever we said we were engaged, women asked to see the engagement ring and admired it in the same way they would flock around a baby. It was part of social expectation in the 1970s. For us life carried on as before, with exams later in the term providing a focus for my worries. Ian and I did not revise together. We were mostly doing different courses. Ian was pure and I was not. In the evenings we would talk about what we had being studying during the day. I learnt about graph theory, logic and number theory and he learnt about fluids, magnetohydrodynamics and elastic media. Explaining a subject to someone else is a very good way to learn and we both widened our horizons. Quantum mechanics was a subject that particularly interested Ian and he had also been to John Polkinghorne's third year course. We had sat together in the second row of his lectures, trying to avoid getting chalk thrown at us, and learnt how to solve Schrödinger's equation and how to calculate the structure of the benzene ring. Neither Ian or myself had taken chemistry O-level, which would have helped us. Strangely Ian had taken Russian instead and had also taken it at A-level, along with double maths and physics. He retains impeccable Russian pronunciation but was never much taken with studying Russian literature. For a while we went to productions of Chekov plays, seeing Uncle Vanya, The Three Sisters and The Cherry Orchard, until we realised that neither of us really enjoyed them. Now we stick to Russian music and operas.

The exams came and went at the end of May. Afterwards, the maths fellows in college, Andrew Tristram, Geoff Eagleson, Graham Dixon and Douglas Gough, hired two minibuses and arranged a day out for the third year mathematicians at Woburn Abbey. We drove through the lions and monkeys in the safari park and, following bread rolls from Fitzbillies and a certain amount of cider drinking, we went on the carousel at the fun fair. It was a great way to end the year. As usual my worries about exams had been unfounded and I graduated with a good first class degree. Both Ian and I obtained places on the Part III postgraduate course and we planned to marry at the end of it. My mother asked why on earth I wanted to do that and told me I must be mad wanting to continue at university. She had never questioned my brother when he decided to do a Ph.D. As far as she was concerned I had sufficient education now, although she did continue to enjoy boasting about her children at Cambridge.

A Maze of Twisty Passages

The college had sufficient rooms to house all undergraduates but Part III students usually lived out. Douglas Gough was responsible for room allocations. I was not keen to move out of college and suggested to him that it would not be safe for me to live out. Since October 1974 the Cambridge rapist had been attacking single young women, entering their rooms by force. For that reason college was not putting female students in outward facing rooms, leading to the anomaly of Mark Manning living in a staircase of women. Douglas thought my reason was original and I was allocated a room in college, on the north side near the Hepworth sculpture facing into a courtyard. Ian had to find digs and spent a term as the lodger of an odd lady near Chesterton Road. She would not allow me to visit and Ian had to live there making absolutely no noise or mess. As soon as a room became available in college he also moved back.

The graduation ceremony took place at Senate House, at the top end of King's Parade, in late June, and was followed by a buffet meal at Churchill. The ceremony itself was an archaic spectacle, as groups of four students, all wearing white bunny fur hoods, were presented to the vice-chancellor by the college praelector, who read his words in Latin from a prompt that he kept in his mortar board. We were told by him that we must each hold one of his fingers with our right hand 'for the magic to work'. As our names were read, we knelt before the vice-chancellor and someone behind us rearranged our gowns so we did not trip as we got up. We were given our degree certificates on the way out and we discovered that we had unpretentious certificates from a prestigious university. Most of us had parents present and Ian and I were no exception. This was where our parents first met. We managed to spend some time saying goodbye to friends who were leaving college and we were bequeathed the Mah Jongg set, as between us we had the largest share.

I have lost touch with most of the students who graduated that day. When I started writing, I began to google names, thinking I might find out what had happened to my contemporaries. First I found that Richard Pinch, from Trinity, who had sat near me in exams, went to work as a senior mathematician, at GCHQ. That fitted with my expectations of how careers might have progressed. Searching for Churchill mathematicians, I found that Peter Cussons, who had been the youngest in my year, died in 2015 after a career in finance. That led me on to think of two Brians who were great friends. Brian Duffy was a mathematician and, following a Ph.D. at Liverpool, I discovered that he became a lecturer at the University of Strathclyde. His friend, Brian Copeland, was an engineer, who like my brother was sponsored by the Post Office. He coxed the men's first eight and died not long after leaving college from some illness that it was thought he might have contracted from the river. Continuing my researches, I found myself quite distressed to discover that Kari Blackburn had committed suicide at the age of 53. I had not known her well but she was one of the very first people I had met in staircase 46 kitchen on my first day in college. I discovered that she had joined the BBC and was director of international operations at the BBC World Service Trust when she died. It is always sad when someone is finding life so hard that they take their own life. I decided that I did not want to know more. I prefer to think of people I once knew living fulfilled and happy lives and shall leave them some privacy. The web is a great thing but I have my doubts about social media where it is too easy to reveal more about yourself than you desire. We have stayed in touch with close friends and still meet up with some of them.

Back in Swansea after graduation I was dropped one morning outside my old school with instructions to go in and thank my teachers. I was not keen on this idea but complied. I found the headmistress was much more impressed that I was engaged to be married than that I had a first class degree. It was disappointing. The unmarried female staff all seemed to be envious. I felt like an oddity wanting to pursue an intellectual life. I did not see my forthcoming marriage as an end in itself but as a prospect that Ian and I would be good for each other, doing things together that we could not do separately. I fear I just confirmed my headmistress's view that going to a mixed college was the best way to find a husband.

I had arranged a summer job at the meteorological office in Bracknell while my father had arranged for Ian to work at the local vehicle licensing office in Northampton. It was thought we would not meet all summer. This was not our plan and we both had free weekends. Most often we met in London. We visited museums, went on the river to both Hampton Court and the Greenwich Observatory, climbed the Monument commemorating the Fire of London and went up the dome of St Paul's Cathedral. Twice Ian's father picked me up in Bracknell and I spent the weekend at their home outside Wellingborough. I was surprised to learn how much Ian's dad knew about the met office buildings. He was working in plant hire and had been involved in the construction of the offices. It was a fine summer which was fortunate for Ian as he had to cycle ten miles to work in Northampton. His job involved mundane administration and filing. The local vehicle licensing offices were in the process of being closed down, as people preferred to get their vehicles taxed at the Post Office or by post to the DVLC in Swansea. I do not think Ian ever mentioned to anyone he was working with that it was my father who was visiting all the offices before they were closed, trying to ensure people working there could find jobs elsewhere in the civil service.

I was working in the experimental labs at the met office, run by Spike Hide, sharing an office with Alan Plumb, a meteorologist who had a Ph.D. on the climate of Venus. It was a great introduction to maths modelling, studying the baroclinic instability in rotating annuli. These were cylindrical vessels full of water heated on the outside and cooled on the inside, designed to model atmospheric circulation with the aim of understanding the motion of the jet stream better. I lived in Crowthorne, just around the corner from Broadmoor prison for the criminally insane.

Part II

Every week the alarms were tested, to help prevent escapes. I walked around the external perimeter, outside the tall brick walls, thinking that living in such a place would probably send me insane, but glad to be protected from the murderers inside. Each morning I would get the bus to Bracknell, reading Solzhenitsyn's books on the way; *August 1914*, *Cancer Ward* and *A Day in the Life of Ivan Denisovich*; more light reading. At the bus station I often saw Chris Rogers, another Cambridge mathematician, a statistician, who was on his way to his summer job at Road Traffic Labs in Crowthorne.

I really enjoyed that summer job at the met office. I would have considered working there full-time but if I had become a permanent employee I would have had to move to a new department every two years, with the expectation I would soon become a senior manager. I wanted to continue with research. During the summer I met a visitor to the labs, Melvin Stern, an American oceanographer, who always had a pipe in his mouth. I would not have believed then that we would work together a few years later.

5. Part III

After a short holiday youth-hostelling in the Lake District, Ian and I returned to Cambridge as postgraduates. Many of our contemporaries had left and we got to know more people from other years. Our lectures now took place in the maths departments. Ian's were in the Department of Pure Maths and Mathematical Statistics, known as DPMMS, and mine were in the Department of Applied Maths and Mathematical Physics, known as DAMTP. Both were rambling old Cambridge University Press buildings off Silver Street, south of King's Parade, that had been adapted, with a lab in the basement of DAMTP. I walked or cycled as the mood took me. My favourite route was to walk through St John's playing fields, following the choir boys on the way to services, continuing through New Court, that was not so new having been completed in 1831, and there I enjoyed watching the young men in towels going to the showers on adjoining staircases. I was glad Churchill had the modern convenience of showers on every staircase. Then I would go straight past the sign saying 'Members of College only' and crossed the river by the Bridge of Sighs. No-one ever stopped me, despite the fact that I could not have been a member of the college. It only went mixed in 1981. The alternative to walking was to cycle past the University Library and over Garret Hostel Lane bridge, which was a lot quicker but far less relaxing, especially as I was still riding the heavy, unstable RSW16 bike. I was thankful that any route that I took was relatively flat and that the bridge provided the steepest hill that I had to negotiate. The flatness of Cambridge did become a problem when we first moved to Bristol. We had both learnt to drive in Cambridge and were not taught how to do hill starts. There was no suitable hill. In Bristol hills were abundant. On an early visit, using the Bristol A-Z map, we took the shortest route from the university to a house we were viewing in Hotwells and went up Constitution Hill and down Clifton Vale. Owning an 850cc bright yellow mini metro, known to my colleagues as the yellow peril, the car struggled. We quickly learnt how to do hill starts and bought a newer red MG metro with a larger engine that was could manage the hills more easily.

Part III is a transitional year before embarking on a Ph.D, mostly taken by students who graduated from Cambridge. In 1975 it still qualified for local authority funding which meant continuing to live on a means-tested grant. It was definitely a masters level qualification, which has now been recognised with the award of a retrospective M.Math. It was mostly taught courses and there were no more supervisions. No-one else from my year at Churchill was taking the applied courses, although Dave Lever, who I had known since my first year, had just become a Ph.D. student in fluids and could sometimes help. The earlier example sheets were replaced with open-ended, and sometimes unsolved, problems but, with much smaller classes, we could now ask questions of the individual lecturers.

Having developed an interest in geophysical fluid dynamics at the met office, I learnt more about the atmosphere and oceans in courses on stratified fluids and oceans given by Herbert Huppert and Adrian Gill. It was from Adrian Gill that I first heard of the greenhouse effect, which allows the long wavelength heat from the sun to penetrate the atmosphere which is then reflected as short wave radiation that is partly absorbed into the atmosphere. Without it the earth would be too cold for us to survive. Now, with the excess levels of greenhouse gases that we generate, we have too much of a good thing. Michael Longuet-Higgins taught us about waves on the surface of the ocean. He invited those of us taking his course to his home and proudly showed us the small waterwheel he had in his garden which supplied his household power. Michael McIntyre explained conservation laws in water waves and the importance of wave action. James Lighthill taught us how fish swim, birds fly and how sperm manage to move at all. Tim Pedley taught us some complicated techniques in boundary layer theory, which later impressed people when I understood triple-deck boundary layer theory and could use the Wiener-Hopf transformation. There were moments when I noticed I was the only woman in the room. Tim Pedley told us we could observe a free shear flow whenever we used the urinal. I would have found it more helpful and less embarrassing if he had suggested watching the stream from a hosepipe when watering the garden. Just for fun I went to a course by John Wheeler on general relativity which involved a lot of manipulation of contravariant and covariant tensors and we obtained the Schwarzschild solution to find black holes. Stephen Hawking was often in the department but was not lecturing. I avoided him as he had a tendency to aim for students when careering around the corridors in his massive electric wheelchair.

As part of the course I took the 'Part III essay' option. The subjects were chosen individually in negotiation with the lecturers and I took the title 'Seismic body wave propagation in inhomogeneous media', from the course Brian Kennett was teaching on elastic media. I generalised material that we had been taught in lectures and it was more of a research project than an essay. Brian Kennett's office was just beyond the Churchill playing fields in Madingley Rise House, where the Earth Sciences was located, and he effectively supervised my project. I had not written any essays since English lessons in school but enjoyed starting the essay with a quote and a picture from Beatrix Potter, 'There was a curious roly poly sound from under the floorboards.' It took me a long time to find an accurate reference for that quote from *The Tale of Samuel Whiskers*, published by Frederick Warne in 1908. It was an appropriate quote as using sound waves to find a kitten is not dissimilar to using seismic waves to locate earthquakes; the topic of my essay. At least that was the connection that I made.

Ian and I used to regularly wander around the grounds beyond the playing fields where both Earth Sciences and the Institute of Astronomy were located. Quite commonly on a quiet Sunday afternoon we would come across Martin Rees, who later became the Astronomer Royal. I guess that finding courting couples was a price he had to pay for working on Sundays. Wandering a bit further we would visit Richard Grant at Kapitsa House on Huntingdon Road. Pyotr Kapitsa was a Russian physicist, who had worked in Cambridge before being detained by Stalin, after a trip to visit his parents. He continued his academic career in Russia, winning a Nobel Prize in low temperature physics, but could not return to the UK. Churchill college appointed him as an honorary fellow, allowing them to house some advanced students in the house he still owned. It was a lovely house, quite a contrast to the modern college buildings, but not so convenient.

My brother married Penelope Horsburgh on 20th December 1975 in Ipswich, with Richard Grant as their best man. Their wedding was held at the Church of St Augustine of Hippo, which I thought a magnificent name for a church, even though I knew Hippo was a place in North Africa and not an animal. I was a bridesmaid along with Penny's sister, Jill, and dressed in blue satin dresses with chiffon sleeves we processed up the aisle behind Penny and her father. The men were all dressed in morning suits and had top hats. They looked smart but rather sombre. I associated morning suits with funeral, not weddings, having previously thought they were called mourning suits. I did not connect them with the joyful top hat and tails of Fred Astaire and Ginger Rogers. I would have been more at home with black tie and gown rather than something that seemed to belong to the Sebastian Flytes and Christopher Moncktons of this world. The reception was held at the private school where Penny's mother was head with caterers supplying a buffet lunch. My parents, Ian and I stayed at an old coaching inn in the centre of Ipswich and returning late at night it all looked rather Dickensian in the run up to Christmas. I was glad we were marrying in the summer.

In the Spring term Ian received an invitation from his old school to a social event for those students from his school currently at Cambridge, plus their wives or fiancées. Girlfriends were not acceptable and the possibility of a same-sex partner was not even considered. Ian and I were engaged, so we accepted the invitation and, with me wearing the engagement ring prominently, went to the party, held in the Wordsworth room at St John's College. I was anticipating meeting some of Ian's teachers, many of whom seemed to be called Dom. It was a rare occasion on which I felt uncomfortable at being the only women present. It was a very stiff and formal affair and we remained unclear why the school had organised the event. Ian had hoped to meet the maths teacher who had inspired his passion for the subject but he was not present. The teachers who had come were almost all Benedictine monks, whose title of address is Dom. It is no wonder I felt uncomfortable in this group of older, nominally celibate, men from St Benedict's School, Ealing, a number of whom have now been found guilty of sexually abusing the boys in their care. Ian was a scholarship pupil at the school, travelling in daily from Bushey in Hertfordshire, and was fortunate to have avoided any inappropriate attention. Not all the old boys from the school had been so lucky.

Until now we had always been examined with papers that covered all the courses that had been taught, not just the ones that we had attended. One of the skills we had needed to acquire was to recognise which questions on a paper came from courses we had studied, although by our third year each question included the name of the course it was examining. There was one question from most courses on each paper, which made for long papers mostly consisting of questions that we could not hope to answer. The examiners who were appointed each year set the questions, often for courses they had not taught recently, using the syllabus published in the Cambridge University Reporter, which the lecturers were supposed to stick to. Sometimes the questions set did not entirely fit with what we had been taught but it made the exams a creative experience. By Part III we were set single papers for each course by the person who had taught it. The papers varied a lot in difficulty. Tim Pedley, who taught the course on boundary layer theory, took a vote to decide whether to set an open book or a closed book exam. I voted for the closed book exam. More voted for an open book exam, thinking it would be easier if we could refer to our notes. They failed to register that it would mean that we would be set a harder paper with no chance of gaining easy marks from bookwork. The rubric on the paper that we later sat stated that full marks could be obtained for a complete answer to one question and there were just two questions on the paper. I remember the question I answered on that paper, which involved the flow of an axisymmetric plume in a stratified environment, like a cooling tower emitting hot air. I did derive a sense of satisfaction as I made it to the end of the question in three hours. I later discovered the content of the question made up the bulk of a recently published paper in the Journal of Fluid Mechanics. I did not have time for the second question. Other papers were more predictable and included some bookwork. Herbert Huppert's paper included a question on the convection of a rotating cylindrical container heated from below. I successfully got to the end of that question and established that rotation makes it harder for convection to start which led me to think that is why hot plates on cookers do not rotate. It surprises me that I can still remember questions from over forty years ago. I guess that my little grey cells enjoyed the exercise once the exams had started and my anxiety had subsided.

I have less memory of how Ian and I made the preparations for our wedding, which was to take place straight after the end of the course. I think I just got on with what needed to be done and assumed that if we had asked for something to be done it would happen. We had decided to marry in Cambridge, persuading my mother that it was more convenient for our relations than Swansea. We considered using the college chapel for the ceremony, but it was not registered for marriages and we would have needed to get an expensive special licence, so we approached Mark Ruston, vicar at the Round Church. We had been going to the Round for a while but I was not baptised and Ian was still nominally a Roman Catholic. We were required to attend confirmation classes and were taught that God is omnipresent, omniscient and incomprehensible and expected to believe all sorts of impossible things. We were told it was our duty to preach the gospel because people would go to hell if they did not become Christian. I certainly did not agree with everything we were taught but I did know that I wanted to be baptised for myself. I still think the gospel is good news but somehow in the hands of the church it often becomes a means of controlling people and leaves people with an unhealthy obsession with sin. Ian and I talked about faith and I discovered the catechism that Ian had learnt as a child. I liked its definition of a sacrament as an outward and visible sign of an inward and invisible grace. Marriage is a sacrament that requires two people to commit themselves to each other in the presence of God. That was what I wanted for our marriage. I also first heard about Vatican II, which had modernised the Roman Catholic church, introducing mass in English and which accepted that there is salvation outside the church. At that time I would have agreed to becoming a Roman Catholic if Ian had wanted it. Denominations were not and are not important to me.

I was baptised with a sprinkling of water at the end of the Spring Term and, at the same time, Ian was received into the Church of England with a handshake, as his Roman Catholic baptism was accepted as valid. Three weeks later, when the Bishop of Ely came, I was confirmed with other students. I was tempted to put my foot down at that. Confirmation is the process by which people take upon themselves promises that have been made on their behalf by godparents when they are baptised as babies. I had made promises on my own behalf just three weeks earlier. As far as I was concerned the confirmation was completely unnecessary but I had to go through with it if we were to be married at the Round. My parents came to that service and afterwards someone came to talk to us. It was Miss Davies, who had been one of my teachers at my primary school, Micklem Junior Mixed Infants School in Hemel Hempstead. She remembered my parents, who would not have changed as much as I had. She seemed so young; younger than most of my lecturers. Now in her early thirties, she would have only just qualified as a teacher when I was eight, yet to my mind I had thought of her as old. She was now teaching in Cambridge and a regular at the Round.

While my parents were in Cambridge my wedding dress was chosen. It came from a shop down Mill Road and satisfied my mother, which was what mattered most. Walking across Parker's Piece towards the dress shop, I saw James Lighthill approaching us as he left the swimming pool. He greeted us, 'Hello Judy.' 'Hello, Sir James,' I replied, surprised that he knew my name, and we walked on. My mother was upset that I had not introduced her but I wanted to keep my university life separate from her as much as possible. My mother favoured having the reception at the Garden House Hotel, which cost at least £5 per head. Eventually we persuaded her that we wanted the reception in college although she was worried it would not be impressive enough. At £1.25 per head she thought it would seem cheap. In the end she was well pleased. With just under a hundred guests, the reception was held in the Club Room. We would have rattled around the main hall, which comfortably seats four hundred people and is the largest in Cambridge. College was only charging us cost price and did not charge at all for the staff it provided, including the head waiter with his gavel. The female staff especially loved having a wedding of members of college. It was excellent value for money and far more impressive than anything we would have had at the

Part III

Garden House Hotel. My new father-in-law enjoyed the occasion too. At that time he was a keen home wine maker, always looking for empty wine bottles to fill. He had a quiet word with the head waiter who showed him round to the loading bay where he found a lifetime supply. We later enjoyed his idiosyncratic home-made carrot wine bottled in old college wine bottles.

The Part III results were announced on 17th June, exactly two days before our wedding. In an ancient ceremony, each year all the maths tripos results are read out by the chair of examiners in Senate House, before the lists are thrown from the balcony into the crowd below. Ian and I waited mesmerised until we each heard our names read out in the list of those who had obtained distinction in Part III. To my astonishment my name was then read again. It appeared that I had won something called the Mayhew prize, jointly with Chris Rogers, the statistician who I had regularly bumped into the previous summer. I discovered this prize was awarded every year to an applied mathematician. I had come top of my year in Part III which should have inspired confidence in me but actually scared me as I still did not believe in my own abilities. I did recall my maths teacher at Hemel Grammar who had thought I was not good enough to do A-level maths. I did realise I had conclusively proved him wrong.

It was after we had set the date for our wedding that we had been told we needed to be in Cambridge for the results, so it was fortunate that we had not chosen to marry a week earlier. Ph.D. places were allocated on the strength of the results. Ian and I parted company as he set off to visit Professor John Cassels, head of DPMMS. The applied students had to meet individually with Professor George Batchelor, founder and head of DAMTP. It was surprising that DAMTP was not established until 1959, slightly before the pure maths department. One might think that Cambridge University would have had a maths department long before 1959 but it is not so. In earlier years people worked independently in their colleges, with joint lectures and exams but no central offices. As a student I had not realised that the department was not as old as the university. It was only when I was invited to its fiftieth anniversary in 2009 that I discovered its history. George Batchelor had worked hard to encourage scientists to work more collaboratively. Not everyone liked the idea. The notoriously introverted quantum physicist, Paul Dirac, was allocated an office in DAMTP, with his name on the door, that he never entered. I enjoyed the fiftieth anniversary celebrations in the newly built Centre for Mathematical Sciences, meeting people I had not seen for some years. The celebrations also included retirement parties for two professors, who had reached the compulsory retirement age of sixty-seven. Both gave lectures looking back over their careers. Tim Pedley was looking forward to retirement, with the opportunity to spend more time bird watching. As Tim's lecture ended, the room filled as Stephen Hawking took to the stage. He made it clear that he was not ready to retire. Work was what gave meaning to his life. Stephen Hawking's position as an icon for science in undeniable. He is as recognisable as Albert Einstein. I hope his legacy is to inspire people to live their lives to the full, learning to live with whatever lies in their way, whether it is physical disability or social pressure that squash people's expectations of what they can achieve.

Back in 1976, I was first in to see George Batchelor and after I had been congratulated I was asked who I wanted to do a Ph.D. with. This was something of a surprise to me as I had not expected a free choice. After some thought I decided to work with Herbert Huppert on a Natural Environment Research Council grant (NERC) and became his first female research student. I did vaguely think of working with Brian Kennett but knew I was not really sufficiently interested in geology. A grant to work on polar studies at the Scott Polar Research Institute with Peter Wadhams also interested me but at that time women were not allowed on Antarctic bases which effectively ruled it out. All sorts of forms had to be completed to secure the funding and I did what was necessary that morning. I was very grateful when George

Batchelor offered to find the referees I needed as he realised I must be busy with the wedding only two days off.

Ian failed to be offered an immediate Ph.D. place despite his distinction. Nevertheless John Cassels assured Ian that he could expect to receive a grant in September on appeal to the Science Research Council (SRC). Ian was hoping to work on problems in mathematical logic with Dr Matthias from Peterhouse, for whom Ian had written his Part III essay. We were happy that we could remain in Cambridge and planned to move into one of the college's Wolfson flats when we returned in September.

It rained on June 19th 1976. It was the beginning of the long hot summer of 1976 and it had not rained for about two weeks but our wedding photos show the rain on the Norman arch at the entrance to the church. My parents stayed at the University Arms hotel, overlooking Parker's Piece with Auntie Edwina, Uncle Harold and Auntie Elsie, my father's Welsh relations. The night before the wedding we had a meal with them all and the Greek waiter wished us many children. Ian and I had managed to squeeze about ten of our friends onto the wedding list, mostly because Ian had only two relations coming, apart from his parents and his brother and sister. David Race, a C.U. mathematician was to be the best man, and Dave Lever and my brother, David, acted as ushers. I had just one bridesmaid, Ian's teenage sister Sue, who had made her own green and white dress. Unsurprisingly Ian's ten-year old brother, Brian, refused to be a page boy. We had decided against morning suits and Ian wore the suit that his father had bought him for his twenty-second birthday. We like to be able to say that Ian got married in his birthday suit. My parents came up to Churchill on the morning of the wedding and I changed in a room set aside by the entrance to the Club Room. I had chosen red and white carnations for my bouquet, yellow and white for Sue and button holes in red and white. Ian almost never buys flowers but he had bought me a bunch of carnations from the market for my birthday eighteen months previously. I was impressed. Rarely receiving flowers I did not have a vase so displayed them in an empty milk bottle. Flower arranging is not my thing. However red and white carnations had become special to us and were what we wanted for our wedding. When they were delivered my mother made it clear she did not approve of my choice and said it was unlucky to have red and white flowers. She refused to let my father wear a red carnation but I managed to hang on to my bouquet. I was used to this sort of response but Sue recently told me how it shocked her. Sue's main surprise was hearing me being told I could not wear my glasses and me pointing out that I could not see without them. Compliments were not part of my mother's vocabulary. However, everything seemed to work as if by clockwork. My father and I got in the limousine to the Round Church and I thought we would be early until I discovered we had to negotiate the one-way system behind the Round so we could pull up at the front. Plenty of tourists were around watching the spectacle. No doubt it made their day to see a quaint British wedding. I wanted to walk down the aisle to Handel's 'Arrival of The Queen of Sheba' but it was beyond the organist's skills so I had to settle for the hornpipe from the water music. As it started I was ready to set off down the aisle but we were detained by the photographer who wanted a portrait of me with my father. Finally we walked down the aisle and I was relieved to be given away to Ian. We used the most modern form of service then allowed, dating from 1928, and to no-one's surprise I did not promise to obey Ian. As Ian says it is harder to love, honour and cherish than it is to obey. The service was taken by one of the associate ministers, Dennis Lennon, who preached on the wedding feast at Cana where Jesus performed his first miracle, turning water into wine. It fits well with what has become my favourite text, 'Jesus came that we may have life, life in all its fulness.' The service ended with a hymn we had specially chosen with the words, 'O perfect love, all human thought transcending. Lowly we kneel in prayer before thy throne. That theirs may be the love which knows no ending. Whom though for evermore dost join as one.' It was unfortunate that the organist had left the tune we had asked for in the vestry and nobody knew the tune from Hymns Ancient and Modern. Nevertheless we have been fortunate over the years and still hope we have found the love which knows no ending.

Ian and I must have been driven back together to Churchill and the reception but it all passed in an idyllic daze. I had to talk to relations that I had not seen for years and Ian was pulled away by his family. I had been given very strict instructions by my mother not to tell anyone about the new job Ian's father was about to take up. He had been running various businesses and his profession on our marriage certificate appears as company director. He had made us guess what he was moving to and where it was, describing the business as a service industry which everyone uses at some point. It took us a long time to work out that he was about to become a funeral director and he would be moving to Ely. It did not seem to me something to be ashamed of. I managed suitable small talk with my relations and the college staff kept me supplied with glasses of wine, which I put down on tables and forgot. We were not the first two college students to marry each other. Jackie Mehra and Peter Cottingham had married the previous summer, also at the Round, but with a self-catered reception in the sports pavilion. That would have been a step too far for my mother, although I had enjoyed the relaxed atmosphere. I was twenty-one when we married and Ian was twenty-two. It seems young now but I found a new freedom in marriage. I made the conscious decision to change my name from Judith Probert to Judy Holyer. I was happy to see myself as part of Ian's family.

We invited both of our tutors, John Knott and Colin Campbell, to our wedding along with their wives. My enjoyment of art had developed while I was at college and, on hearing that we were planning to spend our honeymoon in St Ives, Cornwall, we were told about Barbara Hepworth's studios there. Her Four Square Walk Through sculpture was a prominent feature of the college. Apparently she enjoyed meeting members of the college so it was sad that we were not able to meet her because she had died in a tragic fire in her studios the previous summer.

I was glad when the reception was over and we could set off for St Ives. We spent the first night of our married life in a hotel in Paddington and the following morning took the Pullman train down to St Ives. We had stretched our finances so we could stay for a fortnight at the cheapest room in the Garrack Hotel, a bit of a trek up from the traditional harbour, but we enjoyed good food and wine. It was the long hot summer of 1976 and there was no rain. Barbara Hepworth's studios were already open to the public and the gardens seemed quite familiar as they housed another casting of her Four Square sculpture. The hotel arranged a trip to the Minack Theatre, an outdoor amphitheatre overlooking the sea ten miles or more south of St Ives. Most people went in their own cars but we were given a lift by the hotel owners. We never let on that we had just married though I do wonder now if they guessed. We enjoyed the warm evening sunshine and the picnic the hotel had supplied. The play we saw that night was perhaps not the most appropriate, 'Murder in the Red Barn.'

Most of the rest of the summer was spent working at the DVLC in the car taxation department in Swansea. This was not inspiring work. As a married couple we were not allowed to work together. I sat in a large open plan office dealing with annual vehicle excise tax. There were about ten banks of desks, each with ten people, ensuring all the details and the payment were correct on each application and then 'plonking' the tax disk with a large metal stamp. Most people applied just before the start of the month and we were inundated. I worked quickly and held the record for plonking more tax disks than anyone else, managing over one thousand in a day. My father-in-law was surprised to find a note from me when he received his disk that year, but it was just by chance it had come to my desk. At quieter times there was nothing to do for substantial periods. I took knitting to work but it was deemed too noisy. I was relieved that I was allowed to read while waiting for work to arrive. Elsewhere in the same building, Ian was allotted a green pen to mark up old car logbooks for conversion into the new registration documents. There was construction work going on inside his office so when he cut himself, tearing his trousers on a badly placed metal girder, he sent a minute asking for compensation. We had established the tear could not be invisibly mended and, as impoverished students, we could not afford a new pair of trousers. Ian's request for compensation was rejected as incorrectly written. He had used his green pen; the only one he had. The minute had to be in black. We did get the money eventually but we were left with no desire at all to be civil servants. By then this was the occupation of both my parents. My father was a senior principal at the DVLC and my mother had taken an exam in 1972 to become one of the first VAT officers in customs and excise. When we arrived in Swansea she had just completed a teacher training course for mature students but jobs were hard to come by in South Wales. She taught as a supply teacher for three years with almost two years at Pontardawe School, up the valley from Swansea, but there was no prospect of a permanent position. The opportunity to become a late-entrant civil servant appealed to her, as she was good at mental arithmetic and could do the calculations involved with the 8.5% value added tax without drawing a sweat. I am still inclined to correct people who talk about the 'VAT man'. It is strange how genders seem to attach themselves to some occupations.

6. Doctorate

Returning to Cambridge in September we found there was no Ph.D. place for Ian. That year no SRC grants at all were allocated on appeal, to the embarrassment of Professor Cassels who had never before known of a student with a distinction not getting a grant. It was a bit of a blow to us. Ian signed on as unemployed, which was perhaps not the best start to married life. If we had known earlier we might have looked for places together at another university but I was now committed to my place in DAMTP. For many weeks it was unclear whether or not Ian qualified for unemployment benefit; one week he was told he was and the next week not. The job centre required him to apply for a number of jobs including one at GCHQ in Cheltenham. As required he filled in the application, adding that he had to live in commuting distance of Cambridge, which was an insurmountable difficulty, even though Ian was in the process of learning to drive. Unsurprisingly, he was not asked for interview. I was glad I was not going to be married to a spy. Ian did get some unemployment benefit in the end, which paid for the driving lessons, and not long after that got a temporary job at the Scott Polar Research Institute. The position had not been advertised at the job centre. Ian was approached directly by the head of the Cambridge Computer Labs who had been asked to find someone who could help the Scott Polar digitise masses of data that it had acquired the previous year. A submarine had crossed under the Arctic pack ice at the same time as a plane had flown above, in order to study the pressure ridges that form in the ice sheet. The side-scan sonar data had arrived on long strips of paper; a very large number of them. Ian wrote programs for the department's PDP 10 so that a clerical assistant could use a digital pen to get the data into the computer ready for analysis.

Ian had had a long interest in technology and computers, originally inspired as a teenager by finding a piece of eight hole punched paper tape blowing around a car park. Painstakingly he had worked out how to read it and other paper tapes, although he no longer finds this ability useful. This led to him spending a lot of time in the family garden shed making a computer for himself from designs in a magazine. While I like to say he used valves, he always assures me that he used transistors. His sister mostly remembers the six inch layer of solder that lay on the floor. Unlike Charles Babbage he did manage to get his computer working which, along with his place on the International Maths Olympiad, must have impressed his interviewers when he applied to Churchill as he was offered a place before the entrance exam. On taking the exam Ian became an exhibitioner. When Clive Sinclair produced the first scientific calculator in our first year Ian bought one. Ready-made they cost £30. A kit was available for £16, which was still a large chunk of a £480 grant. The calculator Ian bought became something of a centre of attention to his friends as we typed in 57738 57734 (which read hells bells when turned upside down) and got the battery to go flat as the calculator failed to be able to find the tangent of angles near to 90 degrees. With Ian's position at Scott Polar, he began his transition to becoming a professional computer scientist.

We had moved into the Wolfson flats, close to the college chapel. We were on the top floor in a small bed-sit flat. Underneath the top floor flats were small maisonettes which mostly housed overseas students who had come with young children. Our flat basically had a square floor plan with a kitchen and bathroom in the corners near the front door and a six foot square room in the far corner intended as a study. Every day we had to pull the double bed in and out from under an inbuilt wardrobe that was high on the back wall. It was a very small area for two people. The kitchen had an ingenious rubbish bin with a small hatch in the workbench for us to put waste in and a small door in the passageway outside so that the porters could empty the bins without disturbing us. This seemed like a good idea until one of the flats was broken into by someone climbing through the hatch. Our first experience with the fridge led us to discover that it is not a good idea to freeze cucumbers. We had been given some vegetables from Ian's parents' garden and assumed they would be fine in the fridge. Unfortunately it was set too cold, resulting in limp cucumber. The biggest problem we had in that flat was with the heating which came from a night storage heater. It was expensive to run and ineffective. It stored heat overnight, giving it up during the day, when we were out. We would arrive home in the evening to a cold flat. It did not take us long to stop using the heater. The study was unusable. Initially we had put some books in there but soon had to move them out when they started to show signs of damp. We had a small electric convection fan, a wedding present from my father's cousin, that we used when it was really cold but we quickly got used to waking up on winter mornings to see our breath condensing in front of our faces and to finding the beautiful patterns of frost on the inside of our windows. We were happy in our tiny, cold flat.

Mostly we cooked for ourselves but it was a long way from any shops. Sainsbury's in Sidney Street was most convenient for us but we avoided buying anything bulky that would not fit in our bike panniers. It was a long slog back up to our flat. We did not eat a lot of vegetables. Washing powder was mostly only available in large cartons so I was very pleased when a compact liquid detergent called 'Dynamo' was introduced. I liked its name too as I had studied dynamo theory when looking at how the earth sustains its magnetic field during Part III. I was glad when we decided that we could afford to buy me a new bike. Ian had replaced his RSW 16 in the summer of 1975 when he was working in Northampton. He was now the proud owner of a Dawes bike with five speed gears and drop handlebars. Unfortunately it was not just attractive to Ian and one night it was stolen from the bike racks by the flats. It appeared that someone had come round with a van and bolt cutters. His bike was stolen and mine was left, which did not surprise us. Fortunately we had taken out contents insurance on our flat just two weeks earlier and had included the bikes, so we made money on the insurance that year. Ian was well aware how heavy my old bike was, having had one himself, and we scraped together the money so we could each get new bikes. I acquired a purple bike with a full size ladies frame, five speed gears and drop handlebars. The colour was more important than the name, which I do not recall. Ian kept one ahead of me by acquiring a Claud Butler ten speed model but I was quite happy with my purchase. I found that I could now ride with no hands and keep up with others on my own new efficient bike, and I soon learnt to put the chain back on when it fell off as I changed gears. I enjoyed cycling down the backs and over Silver Street bridge into DAMTP. Arriving at DAMTP I used the back entrance and often met Stephen Hawking at the covered ramp that had been built so he could enter without help. We spent weekends cycling around the Cambridgeshire countryside, visiting Ian's parents in Ely and the tea rooms by the pond in Godmanchester, once venturing as far afield as Haverhill, in Suffolk. We were surprised by a call from the police a few months after Ian's bike had been stolen. They told us that they had found it. Unfortunately all that remained was the frame. It appeared the bike had been stripped for parts and the frame, with an identification number indelibly stamped on it, had then been dumped in the river, from where it had been dredged in an annual clean up. It was of no use to it but we did manage to sell it for £5 to the shop that we bought our bikes from.

At the same time as setting out on married life I started my Ph.D. I was allocated a desk sharing an office with Nicole Rockliff, an Australian from Adelaide who had started her Ph.D. a year earlier. Located behind Seminar Room A, our office was accessed down a corridor where the only other room was the gents toilet. I do not know why we were put together there but it was not for our convenience. I discovered that my reputation had preceded me, for on meeting Nicole immediately predicted that I would complete my Ph.D. before she did. I assumed she would be wrong but she was not. As an initial problem I looked at gravity driven flows entering a two-layered environment. It was a hydraulics problem of interest to John Simpson, who had been a school physics teacher and keen glider pilot. He was performing experiments in the basement of DAMTP as a retirement project using milk for flow visualisation. Modelling sea breezes coming inland on hot summer days, I found I could predict the waves that developed on the top of the colder air. Towards the end of my first year I had to produce a progress report on the year's work with a view to being assessed as to whether I was suitable to continue in the department. It was very pleasant not having any summer exams for the first time in about ten years but I did find it intimidating having to explain my work to Paul Linden, whose main interest was in the experiments, and to Julian Hunt, who looked at my work with the eyes of an engineer. Explaining work to other people is always a very helpful way to come to understand it yourself but I did find that interview frustrating as I wanted to explain with equations and they wanted an explanation in words. I was relieved that I was allowed to proceed to my second year. There were about ten of us pursuing a Ph.D. in fluids in my year and we all, as I recall, eventually successfully obtained our doctorates. I was the only woman in the group and I do not think it was either an impediment or an advantage. Just like everyone else I was an individual. We were all different but conversation revolved around subjects we were all interested in. I was fortunate that sports were not popular with anyone. We often talked about the maths problems we were having, making full use of the square white-topped coffee tables that were placed in the common room in DAMTP. We were encouraged to write directly on their wipe clean surfaces. It became a habit that I have had to break. Coffee shops generally object if you start to write on their tables, unless there is a sheet of paper or a laptop between hands and table.

As part of our training we all had to give a seminar in the first year to whatever subgroup we were working with in the department. The main departmental seminar in fluids was held at 4.30pm on Fridays. This was preceded at 3pm by a seminar of the geophysical fluid dynamics group, at which I was to speak. I was normally at the back of the main seminar as I had become the departmental projectionist, a job always given to a first year Ph.D. student. I was adept at showing slides, changing bulbs on the overhead projector and mounting films for projection. I was quite disturbed at the thought of moving to the front and over prepared my talk for the GFD group. I did not want to find myself stuck for a word and wrote out what I was going to say verbatim. We could choose to speak on any relevant subject of interest to us. I am not sure if I was ahead of my time but I chose to speak on climate change. I had found an atmospheric model that showed climate flipping from hot states to cold states and back again over geological periods of time. Feedback effects from ice and clouds meant that large changes could happen comparatively quickly. The talk would have been better if I had not just read it out. In later seminars I would just use brief notes and overhead slides to ensure I covered the necessary material. This was the norm amongst seminar speakers in applied maths. It made for more interesting talks that were easier to listen to and absorb. I notice now that seminars in arts and humanities are most often read papers and feel that the presence of the speaker is almost unnecessary. It is very hard to assimilate new ideas without the pauses that come in normal speech. If I am reading an article myself I can stop and reflect when I find something hard to understand. In a seminar I want an overview of whatever is being studied so that if I want to I can go away and look at it in more detail later. Perhaps I am just prejudiced but I still find it much easier to fall asleep in a theology seminar than in a maths one.

Ian did not reapply for a Ph.D. place for 1977. He was reasonably content in his work and had come to the conclusion that working in mathematical logic was too risky both in terms of actually getting a doctorate and of getting a job later. In the summer of 1977 I went up to Newcastle University for a three week study school on rotating fluids, funded by the SRC, and did not see Ian for three weeks. Nicole Rockliff came too, as well as a few of us from Cambridge making a group of about fifteen students from around the UK. We worked hard during the weekdays and played hard in the evenings and weekends. I had a great time ice skating at Whitley Bay, being kept upright by John, another recently married student having fun away from home. We all went up to Hadrian's Wall, visiting Housesteads Roman Fort, and I struggled to keep up with Bruce Morton, an Australian oceanographer who was also teaching us, as he hurtled along the wall itself. At the start of the final week, returning from a walk down the bleak Northumbrian coast to the remote silhouetted ruins of Dunstanburgh castle which ended with a cream tea in Craster, I was told that I needed to urgently call Ian. This was not easily done as we did not own a phone. I had to get the college porters to find Ian but eventually we managed to speak. Fearing bad news I was very pleased to hear that, out of the blue, Ian had been offered a Ph.D. place. He was required to decide if he wanted to take it within twenty four hours, hence the urgency. I was quite happy to let him decide for himself, even though it would leave us poorer for a while. Ian decided to return to his studies.

Back in Cambridge I found out what had happened. At home in our flat one Saturday morning, Ian had heard the doorbell and opened the door to a stunning woman with flowing auburn hair. Speaking with an eastern European accent she said her husband was coming and wanted to speak to Ian. When he had recovered his composure he discovered that this was Gabi Bollobás, wife of

Belá Bollobás, a Hungarian graph theorist who had taught Ian in Part III. Ian really had been an anomaly in not getting a Ph.D. place with his distinction but it had been a year of excellent students. Belá had already taken on two of his contemporaries for doctorates. However Belá was always on the look out for good students and remembered Ian when the new year's grants became available. Ian knew now that he wanted to work in the area between pure maths and computer science and Belá would make an ideal supervisor. I was always a bit of a problem to Gabi who enjoyed seeking out potential wives for her husband's introspective students. She was inclined to comment on my clothes, advising me on how to dress more attractively. She was trying to be helpful and I recognised her glamour but it was not a path I wanted to follow. I did fear attracting unwanted sexual attention.

Ian and I had known more or less what we were letting ourselves in for when we moved in to our flat as I had had fluids supervisions in an identical flat belonging to Ann Dowling and Tom Hynes in my second year. Now I found myself following in Ann's footsteps, also supervising second year fluids students, using our dining room table to work through problems, with me sitting between two students. Now a Dame of the British Empire, Ann became a Fellow of the Royal Society and the first female head of the Cambridge University Engineering Department; an illustrious career that I have failed to emulate. Questions from students at supervisions were usually course based so I was surprised one day when one of them asked me how to make royal icing. He had a birthday cake to ice and needed the recipe, which I supplied. I did know the student, Dave Freestone, who was a member of the same bible study group as Ian and myself. The cake had been made for another member of that group, Tom Broadbent, who had been an undergraduate and postgraduate chemist at Churchill, before seeking ordination as an Anglican priest. He was now preparing for ordination at Ridley Hall but spent a lot of time at Churchill. In the end I wished I had iced that cake myself. On interrogation we found out that Dave had adapted my recipe; first adding water, because one egg white did not look like sufficient liquid, and then adding flour because he had run out of icing sugar and the icing was too liquid. One egg white would have been sufficient. The icing had set like concrete. We sawed through the concrete to the cake which had suffered no ill effects. It was no surprise that Dave was a mathematician and not an experimental scientist.

We continued attending chapel and became more regular there than at the Round. With the energy crisis of the 1970s, the underfloor heating that had been installed in chapel in the 1960s had become prohibitively expensive to run. The hopes of Sir John Cockcroft, Master of the college at the time of the building, for cheap fusion power had not come to fruition. It was decided to extend the heating from the Sheppard flats to include the chapel but college was not willing to fund the entire costs. A working party was set up which actually worked using pickaxes and shovels. I discovered I was not very effective at the manual labour but supplied the soft drinks and refreshments while others dug a trench to the chapel in which pipes were laid. We ended up with a fully heated chapel and all future working parties have been a disappointment to me, where more is invariably said than done.

The after service discussion groups continued on Sunday evenings and our flat became a convenient venue. We would boil up a massive pot of rice and chicken or chili con carne and serve it with salad and baguettes. My brother, David, had completed his doctorate and moved out of college to a small house off Milton Road but he and Penny would sometimes come and help out. Richard Cain continued as chaplain but he had also become a follower of Bagwhan Shree Rajneesh (also known as Osho) and wore their orange robes. The services started to include readings from the Bhagavad Gita and the Hindu Vedas as well as readings from the Christian mystics, like John of the Cross, Theresa of Avila and Julian of Norwich, also known as Mother Julian. I appreciated these changes finding that they helped my faith to deepen. I did not agree with everything that Richard said and often thought he was naive. However, about ten per cent of his words seemed profound and he remains one of the holiest people I have known. He had integrity and was not willing to say things he did not believe for himself. I was reminded of him at the fiftieth anniversary of the chapel when the former Archbishop of Canterbury, Rowan Williams, was preaching and spoke of the chapel as a place where honesty is possible. When I thanked Rowan for these words after the service he said he hoped they were true. Rowan is another person that I admire for his honesty, integrity and holiness. As far as I am concerned honesty is essential in faith. I was very sad that the chapel trustees could not cope with Richard's honesty and eventually sacked him from his role with the chapel, leaving him in the odd position of continuing as a college counsellor but unable to take services. With the appointment of Bryan Spinks as college chaplain in 1980, services were led by an Anglican liturgist with an academic interest in the Book of Common Prayer. College chapel no longer felt so open and welcoming. I was glad that by then we had moved out of college and had joined the only church in Bar Hill, which was run as a local ecumenical project and included Baptists, Methodists, Quakers, the Salvation Army, the United Reformed Church as well as Anglicans. It would have been truly ecumenical if both the Roman Catholic and Orthodox Church had been included but that would have required a theology of perfection.

My academic studies continued. Sometime during the second year Herbert suggested to myself and another student, John Heritage, that we should set up a lunchtime study group for our contemporaries to provide a non-threatening venue for us to talk about our research and to invite speakers that we could talk to in more depth. Most of us were already going to morning coffee and afternoon tea in the common room and generally sat together. There was not exactly a seating plan for the room but I did not feel comfortable in groups that included lecturing staff. Drinks were served in cheap green cups from a serving hatch and the fluid dynamicists congregated nearby. Particle physicists and relativists congregated at the far end, where one of Stephen Hawking's Ph.D. students would help him both to drink and to communicate. It was very hard to understand Stephen in the late 1970s, before he had his voice synthesiser, but his students, who spent more time with him, got used to it. At that time he was completely unknown, although I was impressed at his determination to live. I gathered from some of the staff that he could be quite difficult in department meetings where he would be manipulative in order to to get his own way. His determination was both his salvation and his failing. Over the coming years, as his breathing deteriorated, he decided to write a book with a view to funding his nursing care. Before he wrote *The Brief History of Time* he was told to avoid equations as each one included would halve the sales. In the end he included just one. I do not want to take any risks so have included no equations in this book!

Our study group got underway, meeting mid-week. By rotation we bought provisions from Fitzbillies, just over the road, and occupied one of the smaller seminar rooms. I enjoyed learning more about what the others were doing and realised my work was going well, despite always feeling as if I was stuck. Herbert encouraged me to apply for a summer fellowship at the Woods Hole Oceanographic Institution (known as WHOI) on Cape Cod in Massachusetts. This was an intensive geophysical fluid dynamics program lasting ten weeks funded by NOAA, the National Oceanic and Atmospheric Administration of the United States, that supported research that might be relevant to the US Navy. It was known to be very competitive to get in and he suggested that I submit an essay for a Smith's Prize based on my work so far, as it would help support my application if it did well. I was not optimistic but should have known better. I never truly realised that I was a gifted mathematician. When I heard that the results had been posted on Senate House noticeboard, I hurried up past King's College and found that I had won a Smith's Prize. As

I stood there a visiting fluids lecturer from New Zealand came up behind me, congratulated me, and told me that my career as a fluid dynamicist was now established. He enviously told me that a Smith's Prize would be my passport to academia, enabling me to get a job anywhere. I completed my application for the Woods Hole summer school for which Herbert had to write a reference. It included questions about minority status. When I suggested that as a woman I was part of a minority he laughed. There was no positive discrimination towards women. In a way I was glad. I would never like to be a token woman, although people who know me say that I would never be mistaken for a token women. I was by now used to being the sole woman in groups. The Smith's Prize did its work and a telegram soon arrived offering me a place for the summer school. Addressed to 'The Department of Applied Mathematics and Theatrical Physics', I enjoyed the error in the name. I fantasised over Theatrical Physics imagining the study of liquid carbon dioxide flowing across stages and different means of producing lighting and sound effects. It sounded much more fun than Theoretical Physics.

Busy making our plans for the summer, I found myself suddenly feeling ill. Not knowing what was wrong I called in at the doctor's on my way home. Directed by the receptionist to a nurse, she told me in no uncertain terms that there was nothing wrong with me apart from a mild sore throat. With my tail between my legs I continued home and went to the college feast that I was scheduled to attend that night, assuming it was a question of mind over matter. The following morning I awoke feeling no better. Ian could see I was not well and suggested I went to see the college nurse as I was not willing nor fit enough to go back to the doctor's. This seemed like a good idea and proved effective. As I stumbled into her office she told me from the far side of the room that I had German measles. Kindly, I was advised to rest, drink plenty of water and take paracetamol and to stay at home for the next ten days, until I ceased to be infectious. It was known that there was an outbreak of German measles in

Doctorate

Cambridge, yet the previous day I had been treated as a malingerer. I hate to think how many people I had passed the illness onto at the feast. There were large numbers of undergraduates present who were about to take exams. I realised that I should have trusted my instincts and not gone but I wrongly assumed the nurse I had seen knew what she was talking about. I discovered that I had caught it from the husband of a pregnant friend of ours. Peter and Wendy Carlsen were older than us and had just moved out of the college flats into a new house just off Madingley Road. We regularly invited each other to dinner where we showed off our cooking skills and we imagined what it would be like to live in something larger than the shoebox that we were used to. Peter was a South African studying for a Ph.D. in control engineering and his wife was from Guernsey, where she and her parents had run a dress shop. At just over thirty, Wendy was deemed to be an elderly first-time mother so when she also caught German measles she was taken into hospital. Fortunately her baby was born with no ill effects but it was a worrying time for her. As a young child my mother had tried hard to get me infected with German measles but I had never caught it, although I did catch measles, mumps and chicken pox. There were no vaccines for any of these illnesses in the 1950s and, while I do not know how common problems were, our next door neighbour had been born profoundly deaf and partially sighted as a result of her mother getting German measles in early pregnancy. I tried not to let on how worried I was for Wendy and her baby.

Before I had fully recovered from the German measles, Ian and I had to go up to the US Embassy to get visas. I needed a J-1 study visa, as I would be receiving income in the States, and Ian was coming as an accompanying spouse. I am sure I was less infectious than I was at the feast a week earlier although I did feel somewhat guilty at leaving home before my quarantine was up. We arrived in Woods Hole at the end of June 1978 for ten weeks and were planning to travel around the States before returning home at the end of September. The summer program had been set up by George Veronis from Yale and Willem Malkus from MIT in 1959. It has been a great success and still runs with much the same format. A very pleasant apartment, owned by WHOI, had been found for us overlooking the Eel Pond, and we shared it with an American couple. The husband, a mature student who had fought in Vietnam, was on the GFD program with me leaving his wife, Rosemary, and Ian to sort out meals, cleaning and our general living arrangements. The GFD program had quite a mixed bunch of students, now called fellows. Mostly from the US, there were two students from the UK, myself and John Chapman, who was studying at Southampton. One student was from Japan, another had a Chinese background, another was doing a Ph.D at Harvard having left Hungary for the UK when he was eleven and another had been a Vietnamese refugee. I do not know if anyone's place had been allocated on the strength of their minority status but I was certainly the only woman. I still find it strange how few women enter the physical sciences and it is not something that seems to be improving. The annual photo of students and staff in 1978, taken on the porch of Walsh Cottage, shows me in the centre as the only woman on the program. Our leisure time included being introduced to the game of softball which, as far as I was concerned, was much like the game of rounders that I had been required to play at school. There were just ten fellows and generally we were all needed to make a full team. We were not very good at it and lingered at the bottom of the league losing every match but one, when some visiting staff joined our team and boosted our strength. What I most remember about the game is the ball, which I would describe as anything but soft. Landing on the centre of my ribcage when I failed to catch it, I found myself with an extremely large, painful bruise that encouraged me to move out of the way of the ball in subsequent games. After the weekly softball game we would pile into cars and head to the Clam Shack in nearby Falmouth where we could indulge in deep fried clams, with or without bellies. Not exactly health food, we discovered all sorts of seafood over the summer. I developed a taste for lobster dipped in butter, which was a messy business. Often members of staff invited us round to their summer homes. Ed Spiegel's wife was a Cordon Bleu cook, so I was amazed when she served what looked like banana crumble as a main course. This was my introduction to scallops, which I now eat whenever I can. Mike Proctor had a cabin on Crooked Pond where we swam before having a barbecue fuelled by hickory bark and we lingered with our burgers and beer. On the whole I do not drink beer as I hate the taste of hops but I was fine with Bud Light, which can only loosely be described as beer. My introduction to bourbon came with a bottle of Wild Turkey that we passed around as we lay on our backs on the pier watching the Perseid meteor shower above us. Willem and Ulla Malkus were great hosts and I am sure some of the success of the summer program came from the care they showed to the students. Woods Hole is a great place to spend the summer, apart from the times when the sea fog comes in and everything becomes wet and dank. It attracts scientists from all around the world to both the Marine Biology Laboratory (MBL) as well as WHOI. It is said that Woods Hole in summer has a higher density of Nobel Prize winners than anywhere else in the world.

The GFD program begins with two weeks of lectures which are written up by the fellows. In our year the principal lectures were given by Steve Childress, from the Courant Institute of Mathematical Sciences at New York University, on dynamo theory; the study of electrically conducting fluid moving in a magnetic field. These lectures were front line research including unpublished material so we had to keep our wits about us to ensure the notes did not contain errors. Interspersed with the lectures were seminars at which the summer staff introduced topics which they were studying and they tried to encourage us to work with them. Most recently I had been working on large amplitude interfacial waves but I needed to find a different project for the summer. I wanted something that did not require computer power and could be more or less completed in the remaining eight weeks of the program. Most of the problems fell in the realms of oceanography. There was a lab in the basement run by Jack Whitehead that had rotating turntables and I could have become an experimentalist, continuing work on the baroclinic instability, but it was hot and stuffy in the basement. However Melvin Stern, who I had met three years earlier, was a regular on the program and his speciality was salt fingers. He was never without his pipe which produced great plumes of smoke and made his fingers yellow as he kept relighting it. I do not know if that put other people off but he was not a popular choice of supervisor. He was more of a physicist than a mathematician and was hoping to get a mathematical proof for some work he had shown to be heuristically true in 1969. I was attracted to the problem, though felt daunted, fearing it would be beyond me. Nevertheless I started on it. Other summer fellows started other problems and we began our summer of hard work. Herbert, my supervisor, visited for a while but had more important things on his mind as his wife, Felicia, was pregnant. I was lucky that I began to see a way to attack my problem while some of the others floundered and restarted on new problems. By the end of the summer we all had something to show for it. Herbert and Felicia also had something quite tangible, a baby son, Julian Huppert. He became the member of parliament for Cambridge in 2010 yet whenever he was mentioned by the press I thought of him as a baby and toddler. Two members of staff at DAMTP produced children who became MPs. Julian Hunt, who later became director of the Met Office and is now Lord Hunt, is the father of Tristram Hunt, who was a labour MP before becoming director of the Victoria and Albert Museum in London.

Salt fingers had always intrigued me since I had first heard of them during Part III. You may not have heard of salt fingers but they provide an important means of mixing in the oceans, strangely enabling salt to mix more efficiently than heat, despite the greater diffusivity of heat. Imagine you are lying in the hot Mediterranean sun watching the sea. As the sun blazes down, water starts to evaporate from the sea surface. A layer of hot, salty water forms over the colder, fresher water underneath. Now something of a fight sets in. The water is not so salty as to make the top layer heavier than the lower and this is where the salt fingers come in. If you take a blob of hot, salty water and move it down it moves into a colder, fresher environment. Heat diffuses faster than salt so the blob gets colder and becomes a cold salty blob surrounded by cold fresh water so it continues to sink. Similarly if a blob of cold, fresh water rises it enters an environment that is hotter and saltier. It becomes hot and fresh relative to its surroundings and so continues to rise. These two processes result in alternating upward and downward motions that have a square planform when viewed from above. The subject area is known as double-diffusion. Salt fingers were first observed in the Tyrrhenian Sea, part of the Mediterranean Sea, west of Italy, where they typically are one or two centimetres wide, about the size of a human finger. They are an important mechanism for mixing salt in the ocean. Melvin Stern was the first to put this mechanism into a mathematical form after it was first conceived of as an oceanic curiosity by Stommel, Arons and Blanchard in 1956. Lab experiments had shown the vertical salt fingers forming into sharp layers and Melvin had proposed something he called the collective instability of salt fingers to explain this. Slow internal waves cause the vertical fingers to overturn in what is an instability on an instability. This was the problem I spent the summer working on. I managed to formulate a way to study the problem and found a rigorous criterion for when the instability would occur, which involved inverting a 9x9 matrix by hand. I was relieved to have reached the end of the summer with a solved problem which was both publishable and could form part of my Ph.D. thesis. In subsequent years I returned to variants of similar problems. I discovered a new small scale instability that existed on the sides of the fingers themselves which has sometimes been referred to as the Holyer instability. I am not sure I like having an instability of my own.

A Maze of Twisty Passages

Our trip to the US ended with three weeks of travel around the east coast states and north into Canada. We hired a car, bought a tent and a camping guide, and set off. We were given a camping stove and other equipment by Andrew Soward, a lecturer from Newcastle University, who had just ended his sabbatical and was disposing of belongings. We defrayed our costs by asking John Chapman to come with us. Initially he was keen to sleep outside, but after one night under the stars in the woods of New Hampshire, surrounded by unidentified, prowling animals, he asked us to stop at a camping store where he bought a small tent. While our tent was notionally a three person tent Ian was not willing to ask him in to share with us. First we travelled north visiting Montreal and Toronto, marvelling at their enclosed shopping malls, designed for freezing winter weather. Travelling on we found the traffic was getting heavy. It was the beginning of September and we spent hours in traffic jams before arriving at a campsite by Niagara Falls. It was packed and we ended up pitching our tents in the last available space, surrounded by other tents, far away from the entrance to the site and the crowds of hooked-up camper vans. The following day we walked into Niagara and were surprised to find many of the shops and tourist sites closed. It was a Monday morning and we wondered where everyone had gone. The Maid of the Mist boats were still running and we donned waterproof ponchos to sail to the bottom of the falls, getting soaked by the spray. When we returned to the site we found our tents standing almost alone in a vast empty field. It was Labor Day; the final day of the summer holidays. We had had no idea that that was why the traffic had been heavy. We headed on as John was keen to get to New York. Before we left Canada we bought some petrol, which we had learnt to call gas. The first time we had bought gas we had needed to ask for help as we could not find the tank. We had not thought to look under the licence plate. We now filled our tank with the slightly cheaper Canadian gas and drove on down through Pennsylvania all the way to Maryland, with a view to visiting the Smithsonian in Washington the next day. The car did not seem to be going well and we wondered if there had been something wrong with the petrol we had bought. When we stopped we discovered that we had driven over two hundred miles without the filler cap to the petrol tank. We bought a replacement rather than driving back to Canada. We got to New York a few days later and found a campsite just the other side of the Lincoln Tunnel in New Jersey, close to a bus route into Manhattan, where we stayed for a week. There, as well as visiting Central Park, climbing the Statue of Liberty and travelling on the subway, we also met with Joe Keller, a lecturer at Columbia University, who lived in Greenwich Village. He generously took us out to a Japanese restaurant, which was outside our experience but an entertaining experience in itself as we watched the chefs cooking. Returning to Boston for our flights home we spent a few nights staying with one of the other fellows from the summer program, Edgar Knobloch, and his wife, Margaret. They were house sitting at a fine house with a swimming pool in Cambridge, Massachusetts, and we enjoyed the luxury of beds after our weeks under canvas. Now summer was over.

While I had been working in Woods Hole Ian had been getting on with his own Ph.D. work. Now at the end of his first year, it had not been going very well. He had been looking at techniques and reading papers but was still looking for a good problem to attack. While we were in the US we discovered that Rosemary Hart, with whom we were sharing our flat, had parents in New Jersey who lived very close to the Bell Telephone Laboratories, where Garey and Johnson worked on problems at the interface between graph theory and computing. Ian knew of them from his reading in Cambridge and managed to arranged a visit. He enjoyed being shown around the labs and I am still envious that he has visited their anechoic chamber. More importantly for Ian he was given access to a prepublication copy of Garey and Johnson's 1979 book *Computers and Intractability: A Guide to the Theory of NP-Completeness*. At the end of this book there is a list of unsolved problems. Ian studied this list intensely looking for something that was both interesting and tractable. In the end he decided to attempt to look at the edge colouring of graphs. It was not a problem with the same public interest as the four-colour theorem and Ian was only hoping to show edge colouring was NP-complete, which is almost like proving it is a difficult problem. This is not the place to go into a detailed description of Ian's Ph.D. work but suffice it to say that an NP-complete problem is one that cannot be solved in polynomial time. The classic example is the travelling salesman problem; where the salesman (or woman) has to visit a number of places minimising the total distance travelled. There can be no polynomial algorithm that will find the best route. Back in Cambridge, Ian's work became more focussed as he searched for a means to attack his new problem. While attending a scientific program on graph theory at the Oberwolfach Maths Institute in Germany, Ian met Robin Wilson, who was working at the Open University, and was helpfully given a prepublication copy of a paper that enabled Ian to use Boolean logic gates to show his problem was equivalent to something that looked more like a computer problem. At Easter there was a graph theory conference in Cambridge and Robin Wilson, his wife Joy, along with their four year old twin daughters stayed in one of the downstairs Wolfson flats so I met them. Spouses were invited to the conference dinner, held in Trinity College, so I went as well as Joy Wilson, who I sat next to. Robin Wilson drew attention to himself by wearing extremely brightly coloured socks which I did not then know were his trademark. As we looked around the hall at the pictures of past Masters lining the walls, I discovered that Robin and Joy seemed to be well acquainted with Rab Butler and, as they talked about their daughters imitating their grandfather by blowing bubbles from pipes when they were on holiday on the Isles of Scilly, it gradually dawned on me that Robin Wilson was probably the son of Harold Wilson, the former prime minister. When we got home I asked Ian why he had not told me but he had just assumed that I already knew. Eventually Ian proved that edge colouring is NP-complete and is in that technical sense a hard problem. He submitted his thesis in 1980, three years after he had started and successfully obtained his doctorate.

My mother retained her interest in my life, watching the papers for anything relating to Cambridge. When I mentioned Robin Wilson to her she immediately knew he was a mathematician and was also astonished that I did not know he was Harold Wilson's son. She did surprise me one day by sending a cutting from the Western Daily Press, a local South Wales newspaper. Apparently the Tenby lifeboat had been launched with a view to rescuing a gentleman seen in the water near Caldey Island. It reported that he had sent them away saying he was just out swimming around the island. The article referred to the gentleman as a Mr Lighthill, a teacher from Cambridge, and then went on to call him Sir James Lighthill, a professor from the University of Cambridge. It implied the gentleman was being extremely foolish. I pinned the cutting on the noticeboard outside Stephen Hawking's office and it caused much amusement in the department. No-one discovered who had posted the article which amused me. Not many people knew that I had connections with South Wales. At the time Professor Sir James Lighthill was the Lucasian Professor of Mathematics, a chair dating back to 1663, which was the chair that Stephen Hawking held from 1979, after Sir James moved to become Provost of University College, London. Sir James was an extremely strong swimmer and regularly swam around islands, sensing which direction the currents ran. It is very sad that this hobby led to his early death at the age of 74 in 1998. Swimming around Sark in the channel islands he failed to return to his wife, Nancy, who was waiting on the beach. The autopsy showed a congenital heart defect, which had not prevented him from swimming around the same island previously. I was glad he had died doing something he loved. He lived life to the full and remains an example to me of how to live well.

A Maze of Twisty Passages

During the Autumn Term I became ill with glandular fever. The college nurse was again very helpful and by resting much more than I was used to my energy levels were more or less back to normal by Christmas. I now had enough material to start writing up so I got quite a lot done while resting. It was arranged that I would give one of the main seminars on the work I had done on interfacial waves. I had been able to show that having air above a water surface increased the height of the highest wave by two percent, which may not sound much but Michael Longuet-Higgins had always assumed the air density had a negligible effect and had been busy doing calculations of increasing accuracy to get results to many decimal places. His work had a spurious accuracy that was not physically applicable, and my work showed where his assumptions broke down. I was using different techniques to him and could also consider waves at any interface, however large or small the density difference, such as between oil and water or cream floating on top of coffee. I liked to say I studied liquid interfaces as I swirled a glass of wine.

Most commonly the Friday afternoon seminars were given by external visitors and it was rare for any of the graduate students to give a presentation. It was an honour to be asked but I did agree with fear and trepidation. Sir James Lighthill was notorious for sitting in the second row apparently asleep and paying no attention to what was going on. He would then ask really incisive questions that more than once led to the complete collapse of the speaker as they realised they had made a fatal assumption in their calculations. I made sure that I was prepared for any questions so when Sir James suggested that the highest wave should have a sharp corner I simply and straightforwardly replied 'No!' before going on to explain why I was correct. Fortunately for me he understood and accepted my explanation. Paul Linden, a lecturer who was present, enjoyed watching the encounter and described it as the irresistible force meeting the immovable object. Herbert suggested I should have been more tactful and rather than saying 'No!' to Sir James should have said, 'That's an interesting question.' He feared that Sir James would feel humiliated but, in fact, Sir James seemed to value me more for being able to stand up to him. When he left Cambridge for University College London I was the only graduate student, apart from his supervisees, that he invited to his home for his leaving party. I was glad of his support.

I spent the Lent Term completing my thesis. I mostly wrote it out by hand before typing it into the IBM 370. I had decided not to type straight into the computer after someone from the year above had lost an entire week's work when the head crashed on one of the hard disks and he lost everything he had written since the last backup onto tape. My thesis included a lot of equations which it was not feasible to type in, as the printers did not have the character fonts for Greek letters and other mathematical symbols such as $\int$ and ∞. I decided to write in the equations by hand. Now it is much easier and I have often used a program called LaTeX to typeset equations. It does have a small downside. When looking for commands I have injudiciously typed latex into a search engine. I do not recommend doing that unless the parental controls are on! Covering problems in nonlinear dynamics, the thesis was not light reading with a lot of manipulation of equations. I fear it could be used to generate either headaches or to induce sleep. The first chapter covered the work I had done on gravity currents, the second covered interfacial waves, the third had the work from Woods hole and the last chapter looked at some general stability problems of internal waves. Herbert was happy with it which was a sign that it was ready to submit.

I started to apply for Junior Research Fellowships in early 1979. These are postdoctoral positions within a college usually for a fixed three year term. I applied to several colleges; Clare, Downing, Girton, and Kings as well as Churchill, using much the same application to each. Trinity college was advertising its fellowships as open to women but this was rather notional as applicants also had to be graduates of Trinity. Belá Bollobás, Ian's supervisor and a fellow of Trinity, has always said I should have gone to Trinity but gender reassignment has never been part of my plans. The application process included asking what research I would do in the next three years and what its outcomes might be. To me that is not research. If I know the outcomes it is not research. I stated what I had done so far and that I planned to do more of the same. This did not seem to put people off. Every year the colleges rushed to be the first to interview prospective Junior Research Fellows. In 1979 the first to interview was Downing College and I was on the shortlist along with about ten others, each from completely different research areas. It was a strange interview. Chaired by the Master, Sir John Butterfield, any fellow of the college could participate so I was sat at an oval table surrounded by about forty fellows, all male. The college already had one female fellow but she was not present. With no specialists from my area, I found myself describing salt fingers and it did not seem to go too badly. The same evening all the candidates were invited to high table. This was clearly also part of the interview process. As we gathered in the SCR I discovered the interviews had run into a problem when one candidate had been asked what he could tell them about frogs. Unfortunately they had their notes in the wrong order and the general relativist that they were interviewing was most perplexed. As the only woman present I was seated next to the Master. I did not find it a relaxing occasion as we talked of Sir John's research in diabetes and of my plans. When we retired to the SCR I was offered some Madeira and the only thing that entered my head was a Flanders and Swann song. It was probably not wise of me to mention it. It is a song that speaks of an older gentleman seducing a young lady by offering her Madeira, which, according to the song, is very much better than beer. As night comes he puts out the cat, the wine, his cigar and the lamps and the lady awakes with a beard in her earhole that tickled and said, 'Have some Madeira, m'Dear!' I liked the category confusion of the song but, I fear that in mentioning it, I came over as feeling insecure in the panelled splendour of the senior common room of Downing College. I was not offered that fellowship although, as far as I know, everyone who was interviewed that day at Downing was elected to a fellowship somewhere.

A few days later I was invited to the office of Michael McIntyre in DAMTP to meet Shôn Ffowcs Williams, the Rank Professor of Engineering. He was in the process of starting up a research company with a view to undertaking government work that, for security reasons, the university was unable to host. He was looking for someone to study novel methods to detect what I soon learnt to call self-propelled underwater vehicles, more commonly known as submarines. Unsure of an appropriate salary he asked Michael what he earnt and offered me a job at that salary on the spot. At best I could say that I was discombobulated and in something close to a state of shock. He was offering more than twice what I could expect from a research fellowship. I could tell that the work would be interesting but was unsure how I felt about defence work. I was very uncertain what to do. However it felt like an offer that I could not turn down and a few days later I accepted. Intuitively I trusted Shôn Ffowcs Williams, whose Welsh lilt and jovial personality appealed to me. I have never felt that trust was misplaced. Research fellowships would still be open to me. My first choice of college would have been Churchill but it had not yet shortlisted. I was told that William Hawthorne, Head of the Engineering Department and Master of Churchill, was not keen on either Shôn or his new venture. It did not seem wise to wait to see if Churchill would still consider me so I was happy when invited to an interview at Girton College.

A Saturday morning in early 1979 found me searching for the Mistress's flat in Girton. It sounded vaguely salacious asking the way. I am still looking forward to the day when Girton appoints a male Mistress. I think it has an even better ring to it than having a female Master, as Churchill now does. Here the interviewing panel was formed of just six people. They were not just fellows of Girton and included the astronomer Martin Ryle, who had shared the Nobel Prize in Physics with Tony Hewish. This interview must have gone well as I was offered the Hertha Ayrton Research Fellowship. I withdrew my applications to the other colleges and got myself ready to join a formerly all female college, that was about to admit its first male undergraduates. I discovered Hertha Ayrton had been a prize-winning mathematical physicist at the end of the nineteenth century and had been one of the first students of the college.

My thesis was now complete and, after a marathon session with the photocopier, I got it bound in yellow, the brightest colour that was available, with 'The Motion of Stratified Fluids' and my name, 'J.Y.Holyer', printed on the spine. I felt quite proud of it. I waited until the first day of the Easter term to submit, which was the first day regulations allowed. I could not submit until the beginning of my ninth term of study. Examiners were appointed. Steve Thorpe, from the Institute of Ocean Sciences (IOS) in Wormley, Surrey, was to be my external examiner. The IOS had a very unlikely location, in premises dating back to World War II that were a very long way from the sea. We used to joke that they were perfectly placed to cope with sea-level rises. More sensibly it has now moved to Southampton where research vessels can dock alongside. James Lighthill was appointed as my internal examiner, despite the fact that he had moved to become Provost of University College, London, and was living in Gower Street. The viva took place on the second floor of DAMTP. It began with Steve Thorpe questioning a statement I had made. It was most gratifying when James Lighthill showed him why I was correct. There were a few typographical errors but I knew I had passed when Sir James told me that my thesis could now join the others in the library and become a bible for future research students. He was inclined to exaggerate my abilities!

7. Fellow

In April 1979, following a short holiday, I started work at Topexpress Limited as one of the first two employees at its new offices at 1, Portugal Place. Choosing a company name is hard. Shôn Ffowcs Williams had joined forces with Jack Lang, a computer entrepreneur, and the name was chosen from those available at short notice from Companies House. Shôn's expertise was in acoustics and noise reduction. He had been a consultant with Rolls Royce on the Concorde engine and one of the projects the new company would be working on was the active control of sound. High frequency noises are absorbed by insulation leaving the problem of the lower frequencies. Actively controlling sound is done by measuring the sound present and then adding more sound that is out of phase with the sound already present. The phase is important because if it is in phase it will simply make things noisier. Using the technique, known as anti-sound, the new company was working with British Gas to reduce the background noise generated by the gas pumping station at Duxford. We batted around various possibilities for names for our new company. Sound Services seemed good until we registered its abbreviation. It was unlikely the Ministry of Defence would want to work with the S.S. Other names we thought of were already in use. Topexpress had been a dry-cleaning company that had stopped trading and we quite liked the way it implied fast, rapid service so we retained the name.

A Maze of Twisty Passages

Topexpress had two wings; one doing scientific research work and the other marketing the Cambridge Ring, a networking protocol that seemed to be technically superior to the now ubiquitous Ethernet, and the name suited all the parts of the business. Topexpress grew quite quickly and about eight of the scientists soon moved into offices premises opposite Magdalene College, where La Margherita restaurant is now located. With solid oak floorboards and a sloping floor, I was inclined to find myself drifting into the lower left-hand corner of my office. In an idle moment I timed how long it took a pencil to roll across the floor and estimated there was a five degree slope to the room, which is really quite extreme. The computer scientists remained in Portugal Place along with two secretaries and a business manager. Liz Acton, an engineer working on the inflow to jet engines, was in the office adjoining mine. She had an odd disagreement with the Post Office when they installed her telephone. Having ordered the phone as Dr Elizabeth Acton, they wanted to know if she was Dr Miss or Dr Mrs. They persisted, claiming that they needed to know which to use so they could address the bills correctly. She persisted, pointing out that to be correct they should send the bills to Dr Acton. It did not get sorted out until the local paper got involved. I would have hoped the situation would be better by now but I regularly have difficulties with shops and utilities assuming that I am male because I have signed something as Dr J.Y. Holyer. If I do not use a title at all they usually invent one. I always published academic papers as Judith Y. Holyer to give people a chance of recognising I am female, although some people still seemed to manage to refer to me as 'he' when referencing my work. I think I discovered part of the reason when showing a Russian oceanographer, Konstantin Fedorov, around the CSIRO labs in Hobart. We had been introduced but, as I showed him the long tank we were using to model double-diffusive interleaving, he realised that I was unusually well-informed about the experiments and asked me again what my name was. When I replied 'Judy Holyer', he asked if that was the Judith Y. Holyer who published in the Journal of Fluid Mechanics. I discovered that he had thought Judith was a man's name! We sat and drank tea together, both of us registering that our colleagues thought we drank an awful lot of sugary tea as we both used dissolved sugar in our experiments to model heat. I was ordering 50kg bags of sugar and 30kg bags of salt regularly. I guess it seems logical to be using salt to model the salty oceans but we needed the sugar too as it was much easier to control that than trying to maintain a temperature gradient in a laboratory tank.

During the summer of 1979 the Rubik's cube first made its way to the UK from Hungary. It did not come under its own power but was imported on a small scale by David Singmaster, an American graph-theorist working in London. Ian knew him and it was probably a good thing I was away when the first one arrived. Returning from an acoustics meeting at the Max Planck Institut für Strömungsforschung in Göttingen, I found Ian not gone to bed until 4am the previous night. He had been determined to solve the puzzle before I got home and he greeted me sleepily and unshaven. Later, ways to solve the puzzle were published by Singmaster and others but in 1979 you had to work it out for yourself. With Ian's help I managed to complete it quickly, although I very much doubt I could do it now. We bought several batches of ten from Singmaster which we mostly sold in Cambridge, though we also sold three to Ken Chandler, who had helped with my Cambridge entrance exams. That year Ken did not send out his Christmas cards until February. He took longer than Ian to solve the puzzle, two of which he had intended to send to his nephews as presents. Determined to solve it, he started by making a few moves that he could undo but as he failed with the first, the second and then the third he found he had to solve the puzzle starting from a random configuration. Now the Rubik cube is ubiquitous and its solution is easily found with an Internet search. Just recently I was sitting on a London tube train watching a young man trying to complete it in under forty seconds. It was an exercise in dexterity rather than thought. We were surprised at how quickly it became very popular and how its popularity endures.

After three years living in the Wolfson flats, we moved out on 1st October 1979 to a small detached house in Acorn Avenue, Bar Hill, a new village being built to the north-west of Cambridge. We had lived very frugally, never eating out and saving any money we received from supervisions. Despite an interest rate rapidly approaching fifteen per cent, we managed to get a deposit together and, with my new salary, could just about afford to pay the mortgage. We had no help from either set of parents so it was quite a commitment but neither of us wanted to waste money on rent. The college flat had been cheap but, although we had managed to negotiate extra time in the flat over and above the usual fixed three years because we were both Churchill students, we were keen to have a little more space than the bed-sitting room gave us. The house cost three and a half times my annual income which gives an idea of house price inflation. The mortgage payments, however, were a good half of my salary and Ian was still on an SRC grant so with extra bills we had no money to spare. In those days it was easier to save for a deposit but mortgages were more expensive. Now house prices are so high relative to income that it is very hard to save for a deposit without family help but, once you have your own home, it is almost always cheaper to pay a mortgage than to rent. It seems very odd to me, if not immoral, that it is now possible, for those with the means, to buy property with a mortgage and to rent it out at an amount that covers the mortgage and all expenses as well as a hefty profit, quite apart from the capital gain in value. Perhaps it is just another example of the old maxim that the rich get richer and the poor get poorer. The system seems to work that way. We continued to keep our living costs down, not owning a television or a car. When we moved in we used garden chairs and a picnic table in our living room along with two strange green sling back chairs that Ian's father had in his garage as relics from the hippy era. Our only purchases were a new bed, a fridge freezer and a very up-to-date off-white, shaggy-pile carpet in the living room that we had to rake regularly. We would cycle down the A14, past the slip road onto the M11, into Cambridge although we gave that up after a couple of months.

One Sunday afternoon we were cycling past the crematorium, I was out in front of Ian and everything seemed to go into slow motion as I saw a lady step out onto the dual carriageway without looking, straight into the path of a car that was towing a caravan. We laid our bikes on the grass verge and a number of cars stopped too. An ambulance soon arrived and the lady was taken off to hospital. Until I put them right, the police assumed that the lady in the road had been on one of the bikes. They knew the dangers of the road. I had to give a statement and was asked for ID. Finding my name was Dr Holyer, they asked if I had rendered medical assistance. I had to explain that I was not that kind of doctor and it would not have been in the best interests of the lady for me to help her. We decided to avoid cycling along the A14 and took to using the bus whenever we could. At weekends and in the evenings, when buses were infrequent or non-existent, we still cycled but we looked forward to the day when we could afford a car. We hoped the lady who had been taken to hospital was OK.

I received my doctorate in October 1979 at a ceremony at Senate House. Earlier that week I had seen that the TARDIS, looking very much like a police box, had landed outside the Baron of Beef pub near our offices, so had realised that filming was going on for Doctor Who. As we walked home from the degree ceremony over Garrett Hostel Lane Bridge we saw a film crew walking towards us, including Tom Baker who, with his long knitted scarf, was fully kitted out as Doctor Who. As I stared at him, he stared back. I guess it is not every day that you bump into someone in full academic dress, even in Cambridge.

I joined the fellowship of Girton College at the start of Michaelmas Term 1979, at the same time as its first male undergraduates. There were two new Junior Research Fellows, myself and a pure mathematician, Peter Webb, who was an extra appointment because I was not taking the money that came with my fellowship. After signing the book where fellows names were recorded we entered hall for a formal dinner, where I was seated next to Mary Cartwright. She spent a considerable amount of time telling me about the problems she was having with her household drains. I might have been fooled into thinking she was an uneducated, eccentric, elderly lady had I not already heard of her. Dame Mary Cartwright was a former Mistress of the college and had also been the first female mathematician elected to the Royal Society. She had worked with John Littlewood on some nonlinear differential equations that were used to model radar and radio signals and used them to study what later became known as chaos theory and the butterfly effect. She was ahead of her time and is not as well known as she should be, even amongst mathematicians.

As a fellow I attended Governing body meetings which, unlike most colleges, included former heads of the college, so two former Mistresses were usually present. At the first meeting I went to there was a prolonged discussion as to who should be allowed to attend. The college had bye-fellows who were usually doing some teaching for the college but were not formally fellows of the college, with the rights and responsibilities that came with a fellowship. They were asking for permission to come to the Governing Body meetings. As the youngest fellow present, the Mistress asked me whether or not I thought that bye-fellows should be allowed to attend. My response was rather over blunt. I said that if they wanted to come they should be welcomed but that I hoped the business was generally more interesting. Some did come to subsequent meetings and discovered that they had not been missing much. The college had only just gone mixed and I picked up on the dissent it had caused. With so many colleges now admitting women, Girton felt it was harder to attract the best candidates and its standards were falling. Certainly Girton had held no attraction to me as an undergraduate when there was the opportunity to apply to a mixed college. A former Mistress, Muriel Bradbrook, had clearly been opposed to the admission of men. I recall her saying that it would be over her dead body that men would be accepted in college. She was still alive and well but men had been admitted. Had I been a participant in the decision to admit men to the college, I would have wanted to say that a mixed environment is healthier for everyone. Girton had been established in the nineteenth century to provide the opportunity of a Cambridge education to women who had been unable to get an education elsewhere. Now women were being admitted to Cambridge in larger numbers than ever before, purely on academic merit from schools where girls and boys had been educated to the same standards. I can see no further reason for single-sex colleges unless we want to live segregated lives.

Despite Muriel Bradbrook, I admired most of the female fellows at Girton who were a formidable group. Mary Cartwright had been Mistress for almost twenty years starting in 1949 and kept her peace in Governing Body meetings. She probably had experience of the difficulties previous incumbents could cause. The current Mistress, Brenda Ryman, commuted between Cambridge and London where she worked in cancer research at Charing Cross Hospital. She was more than competent at everything she put her hand to and, although she died at the age of sixty, not long after I had left the college, her obituary speaks of her fitting three lives into her own short life. Most of the older fellows were not married. One exception was Lady Bertha Swirles Jeffreys, wife of Sir Harold Jeffreys, who were jointly the authors of our first year maths text in Mathematical Physics. They were keen musicians and enjoyed entertaining. Lady Bertha had worked on quantum theory in its early days while Sir Harold was a geophysicist. He was born in 1891 and, ten years older than his wife, he was approaching ninety when I first met him. His mind had not aged as much as his body and he was busy preparing a new edition of his book on the earth. He soon had me checking it and I learnt more about tides and their relation to the movement of the sun and moon than I had ever known before. The Severn bore and the high tides in the Bristol Channel were already familiar to me. After we moved to Bristol we used to take students to watch the breaking wave of the bore, which was often obscured by surfers and canoeists, as it travelled from Newent up the river to Gloucester. Sir Harold still went to seminars in DAMTP but he was very unsteady on his feet. He preferred to cycle. I was amazed at how slow he could go and still remain upright. The college had always appointed married women of sufficient calibre but there were not many men who would allow their wives the freedom to pursue an academic career, at least that is my explanation as to why so few fellows were married. Girton college had always had plenty of male visitors and I heard tales of late night visits to colleges, involving climbing walls and evading prowling porters and proctors. Now the college had gone mixed the men did not all have to leave at night, in the same way as women had been able to stay all night at Churchill for the previous seven years. I imagine it helped students form relationships without it disrupting their studies. It had worked for me!

Following the accident I had witnessed I had not expected to hear anything more from the police and imagined the lady had survived. However, six months later I was summoned to appear at her inquest. She had survived her initial injuries but was left in a weakened state which had led to pneumonia. She had been visiting the memorial to her husband on the anniversary of his death and had obviously been in a daze as she tried to cross the road. I gave my evidence to the relief of the car driver who had hit her. He had been travelling with his ten-year old son. It had been a traumatic experience for both of them and the possibility of an inquest or even prosecution had been hanging over him for a long time. I did learn something about witnesses that day, for another witness was certain it was raining at the time of the accident. I was even more certain that it had not been raining. As I was the one outside on a bike I think I was the one who was believed. Neither of us was lying. It had been a showery day and the other witness must have just assumed it was raining. I realised how hard it was to piece together what had actually happened when the accident had happened so quickly. I was glad the verdict was accidental death and no blame was laid upon the driver. There was a bus stop and lay-by opposite the crematorium which encouraged people to cross the road. The crematorium served Ely as well as Cambridge and Ian's father, now a funeral director, had been dashing across the road there to deliver documents but took to driving round after he heard of the accident.

Soon after the inquest, we managed to buy a cheap second hand car from Marshalls, a 1975 Austin Allegro, known for having a square steering wheel. I was pleased that we no longer had to cycle along the A14 and we drove into Cambridge each day, parking at Wolfson Court, a residential site of Girton College, where we kept our bikes. The day we bought the car, Ian drove it home but the following morning it would not start. After we had walked to the petrol station and purchased a gallon of petrol for the empty tank it was fine. The Mistress of Girton was very amused at this. She was a strong proponent of the unworldliness of mathematicians and suggested we had not realised that we had to put petrol in the car to make it go. At the same time we were decorating our living room with woodchip paper to cover over the flaking plaster beneath. The Mistress said she would love to see two mathematicians wallpapering. I assured her that we had purchased exactly the correct quantity of paper, remembering to account for windows and doors, which only pandered to her stereotypes. I learnt to drive on that Allegro car, taking lessons from Marshalls. I became adept at giving bicycles sufficient space. I have complete empathy for cyclists, as long as they stick to the Highway Code and do not swerve from pavement to road and back again with no indication. I did know of a number of unpleasant accidents involving cyclists, and the cyclist usually came off worse than the car driver. This was not universally the case. Outside the Round Church, I once saw a driver open his door directly into the path of a passing cyclist. I feared the worst. Just for once the cyclist won. The bike and its owner were fine but the car door had buckled and would not shut.

Initially the work I did at Topexpress was not classified. I gave a seminar on the generation of internal waves from by a point source at the British Theoretical Mechanics Colloquium the April after I started work. It was retrospectively classified. Apparently I was supposed to deny I had given the talk. This led to some awkward conversations where I must have come across as very forgetful. Most of the work we did at Topexpress was confidential in some way, which meant we quickly received a government issue safe. It required a delicate touch to get into it. With five turns to the left, four to the right and then three to the left, it was easy to misalign the numbers. I was the company expert at getting into it. It has proved a useful skill. My father-in-law was at his wit's end when he was unable to get into his business safe, despite knowing its combination. I went over to his office and opened it with no difficulty.

My research work at Topexpress meant that I needed to use some serious computer power and the company bought time on the university's IBM 370. In order to run the programs I had written, I had to leave my office in Magdalene Street, go down past St Johns, Trinity and Kings Parade to get to the computer lab. There I sat at a well-used teletype terminal to input and run my programs. Written in the Fortran computer language, they met the secrecy requirements that we worked to provided that I did not add comment statements to say what each part of the program did. I wonder now what might have happened if I had uttered the word 'submarine'. I generally had to wait some time for my programs to run and, at a loose end, I started to play Colossal Adventure, a very early text based computer game. Starting in a wood, the entrance to a cave system had to be found and then you moved from room to room, leaving by different compass points. In order not to get lost it was necessary to hand draw a map. The game included two mazes, one made up of twisty passages all different and the other of twisty passages all alike. With an accurate map, one did not get lost in the maze of twisty passages. I did feel somewhat guilty at playing the game at someone else's expense as my time was charged to the contract I was working on, however I had to do something while waiting and writing confidential reports in a public space was not practical. There were some odd items to be found in the caves, of which I was most intrigued by an emerald the size of a plover's egg, never having heard of a plover. Ten years later, when in hospital in Australia, I was very amused to discover that the birds nesting nearby were plovers. I was not amused by the possums rustling in the bushes when I was out walking before dawn, which just scared me. Life then felt very like a maze of twisty passages and escaping the maze that my life had become is my greatest achievement.

I had not considered studying engineering as an undergraduate. No-one had suggested it to me and I had not been aware of it at school as an academic subject. I may have still studied maths as I like to understand systems from first principles and never much enjoyed practicals, but the course at Cambridge was very mathematical. I am quite surprised now that Churchill College did not enquire as to whether I would like to do engineering. It would have been good to have had a short introduction to each of the different fields. I only knew of engineers working on building sites or designing bridges, and did not realise the possibilities of making computer driven robots in electrical engineering or improving the efficiency of planes in aeronautics. As an undergraduate, engineers were always known as 'Wallies', an epithet that did not encourage me to want to become one. By the time I was a postgraduate in fluid dynamics, I was convinced that the low number of female engineers is exacerbated by people, both women and men, assuming that it is not of interest to normal women; an assumption that is curiously resistant to change. Now, at Topexpress, I was often referred to as an engineer. We did some experiments in the basement of the engineering department in a cubic metre tank full of carefully stratified salty water, which we were assured, by the aquarium company that had supplied it, would not break. We purchased an airfix kit of a suitable self-propelled underwater vehicle, weighted it suitably (by adding a motor and araldite glue) and used red and blue food dyes to provide patriotic flow visualisation. All went well until one night the salt finally corroded the joints on the tank and a tonne of salty water was deposited on the floor of the labs. We were not popular, especially with people running electrical experiments. We had the results that we needed and we left quietly.

I enjoyed taking visitors and friends to college guest night dinners that took place once or twice a term and I could eat at high table every night if I wished. I only took my husband once, because it was frowned upon to entertain one's own family too often. I once took my father who was on a residential civil service management course at Cardington near Bedford, at the base where the R101 airship had been built. He enjoyed talking to Alison Duke, a white haired lady who had the delightful title of Registrar of the Roll, which meant being responsible for alumni. I also once took my brother, probably wanting him to be envious. When we had lived in Churchill we had entertained in our flat but now I could impress visitors by taking them to Girton. I was pleased to be able to return some of the hospitality I had received from Willem and Ulla Malkus, in Woods Hole, who were overwhelmed by the welcome they received. They lived most of the year in Cambridge, Massachusetts, where Willem worked at MIT. Willem had been to formal meals before, but Ulla had never before been invited and thoroughly enjoyed the atmosphere at Girton. By now I positively enjoyed meals that started with sherry, followed successively by white wine, red wine, port or claret, and brandy in the S.C.R. for those of a hardy constitution. It seemed to make no difference whether the majority of those present were men or women. Girton's wine cellar was not quite as good as Churchill's but, as I now came by car, I had to restrict my alcohol intake, so I only drank the best wine in small quantities.

Fellow

There were always interesting guests at the dinners. The conversation with one academic visitor to the university moved to mathematics. He was an older German gentleman who worked in the humanities but he expressed a desire to meet Ian when he discovered that my husband was a pure mathematician. This led to us going, one Sunday afternoon, to a very traditional afternoon tea in his rooms with fruit cake and scones. It transpired that he was a great nephew of David Hilbert, an eminent German mathematician known for formulating twenty-three problems at the turn of the 19th century which provided fertile ground for mathematicians and physicists in the twentieth century.

We reciprocated invitations where we could. In return for an invitation to Girton, Jim Woodhouse, who had joined Topexpress at the same time as me, invited me to the annual feast at Clare College, endowed by Samuel Blythe. This was what is known as a scarlet dinner, where those of us with Cambridge Ph.D.s wore gowns with red panels down the front, as well as the usual formal wear underneath. I liked the idea of being a scarlet woman. The meal was a lavish feast with Christmas pudding forming the final course. As the dinner ended, a 'loving cup', a large silver goblet with two handles, was passed from person to person. Filled with wine, we each had to offer it to the person on our left with the words, 'In piam memoriam Samuelis Blythe.' This was the most opulent and unusual college meal I attended in my time in Cambridge. Jack Lang, one of the founders of Topexpress, was a keen cook and would invite friends and colleagues from Topexpress to Sunday lunch. He later ran a restaurant on Midsummer Common, bringing better food to the population of Cambridge.

I was still taking supervisions and the students now came to my office at Topexpress. Coming in pairs, I would find some chairs without wheels and place them either side of me, so that we could work through problems together, with everyone being able to see and no-one's chair moving into the lower left hand corner of my office. The students now came from a number of different colleges around the university and included some overseas students. I tried not to make assumptions but sometimes failed. I was taken aback when one student told me that he came from London, after I had asked where he was from. I had been expecting the answer Ghana, Nigeria or somewhere else in Africa. Prejudices and assumptions that come from stereotyping people will always be around. The best I can do is to try to notice when they happen. One year, at the end of term party for supervisors and directors of studies, I was told that one of the students that I had supervised for a whole term had returned to his director of studies at Magdalene straight after first meeting me to say that he could not possibly be supervised by a woman. He was a public school product and had never seen a female mathematician. He was persuaded to try me out and see how it went. It was a good thing I had not known about this earlier as I might have given him a hard time. I assume he concluded that I was good enough and overcame his assumption that women could not teach maths. At the same end of term party I found myself talking to someone about schools and we discovered we had been in the same class at Micklem primary school, in Hemel Hempstead. She had come a year later than me, having taken a year out, and had also studied maths to Ph.D. level. In fact three girls from my primary school class went to Cambridge to read maths. One came at the same time as me but only stayed one term due to a family death. It was a very average primary school and the three of us had all gone to different secondary schools and did not know each other well. I have lost contact with them now. The changing surnames of my female friends makes it more difficult to stay in touch when contact is infrequent. As far as I know nobody else from my class went to Oxbridge and maybe it was just a coincidence but it must be unusual for three girls from an insignificant state primary school to all go to Cambridge to read maths. I had enjoyed maths at Micklem with Mr Bell, who encouraged those of us who had completed the standard text books by setting us little projects. I recall measuring the heights of all the trees in the school playing fields by using a tape measure, a protractor and a cardboard roll with cross hairs. It was even more fun trying to work out how to get the jumper off Ian Sinclair without removing his jacket. Two others did come to Cambridge from my year at Hemel Grammar. They both had a year out and came to Churchill a year after me, in 1973. David Pritchard had been in the science form at school and read maths. Robert Gibson had been one of the few boys with me in the language form and he came to read history. I did not see much of them while they were students and they both left after their undergraduate degrees. I do not know what happened to David Pritchard but I did meet Robert later at a Churchill reunion. We talked more then and I told him I had been surprised when he had turned up at Churchill, as he had been bottom of the class when I left Hemel Grammar at the end of the fourth year. He had only joined the school at the beginning of that year, having lived in Switzerland or somewhere in Europe until then, and he was bored by our lessons. The following year he did much better, which explained his arrival at Churchill. When I met him he had just retired early, which encouraged me to do the same shortly afterwards.

After two years at Topexpress I was starting to get frustrated that I could not talk to anyone about the classified work that I was doing. Later, when studying ethics as part of a theology degree, I wrote an essay which argued the case that there was no moral justification for nuclear deterrents, ending with an elephant joke, which goes,

'Why do elephants paint their feet yellow?'
'So they can float upside down in a bowl of custard without being seen.'
'But I have never seen an elephant floating upside down in a bowl of custard.'
'That proves how effective it is.'

I do not believe that nuclear deterrents work and fear the disaster that would be caused if there are used. At the time I had not considered my moral position. I justified the work to myself by saying it was for the defence of our country and that if I did not do the work then someone else would. I no longer think that true. When I saw an advert for two lectureships in applied maths at the University of Bristol I decided to apply. Such adverts were very rare in the early 1980s. The previous year there had been just one lecturing post in applied maths in the UK and these were the only two in 1981. I heard later that about one hundred applications were received from qualified candidates. The positions had come about because one professor at Bristol had taken early retirement and another, Keith Moffatt, was returning to Cambridge. At my interview I was asked if I could describe my research, to which my answer was, 'No!' I did not want to be prosecuted under the Official Secrets Act. I had been expecting the question and I talked about my Ph.D. work and future work I might undertake. One of the members of the panel did know of my recent work as he was a consultant to the project I was working on and my answer did not seem to affect me negatively.

I recall that the interview took place on 30th March 1981. Two days later I had to attend an important meeting at the Admiralty Marine Technology Establishment in Bushy Park, Teddington. I remember the date of the interview because the meeting at Teddington was on April Fools' Day, 1st April. I arrived with some trepidation. I knew that Philip Drazin, head of the Applied Maths group in Bristol and an external consultant to my project, would be present. He had been on the interviewing panel. Just before the meeting started he told me that I was being offered a lectureship at Bristol. He also told me that the panel had not yet decided who else would receive a job offer, so I knew that I was their first choice. Our meeting then started with the chairman proclaiming that nothing that was said in that room could be repeated outside. The proscription seemed to include my job offer. The whole day felt utterly surreal. I have attempted to apply some common sense as to what I can and cannot say about that day. At lunch I asked Shôn Ffowcs Williams if Philip Drazin might have been playing an April Fool when he had offered me the job. Shôn reassured me that no jokes were being played on me. The meeting continued into the afternoon with its continuing cloak of secrecy. It was as a result of that meeting that when travelling in the U.S. a few years later some scientists would tell me that they had read various reports and papers of mine. A link with the U.S. had been made, although I was no longer party to the work being done. As we sped back to Cambridge in Shôn's Porsche, he seemed genuinely sorry that I would be leaving the company.

In some ways I too was sad to leave Cambridge and Topexpress. It had been nine years since I had arrived as one of the thirty women at Churchill. I received various gifts at a leaving party at Topexpress, including a box of Romeo y Julieta Cuban cigars that were one of Shôn's indulgences. I passed those on to my father, who was also a cigar smoker. Our office manager, David Baldwin, gave me a pen and ink drawing of the Wills building in Bristol that had been a gift to his grandfather when he was butler at Dyrham Park, near Bath. It was time to move on.

8. Lecturer

My appointment letter stated that I was to start work as a lecturer in the School of Mathematics at the University of Bristol on 1st September 1981. This was the day after the August Bank Holiday and I arrived bright-eyed and bushy-tailed at the department on the appointed day. I tried to find my way in but the entire building was locked. Nobody had thought to tell me that the university closed for two days for any bank holiday that occurred out of term. Apparently I should have known, because it was the same every year. Three new lecturers had been appointed because of the strength of field of applicants and, because two professors were being replaced, it was still a saving in salaries. By the end of our first year the three of us were all frustrated by the things we had been expected to know without being told and produced a booklet listing the things we had needed to know, just in case any new staff were ever appointed. On my abortive first day, I decided to go for a walk round Bristol, hoping to bump into Ian, who had secured a job in Bath starting the following day. The hills of Bristol were obviously a shock to my legs as by the end of the day I was limping. A few days later I took myself off to a doctor's surgery and, after a trip to casualty, was diagnosed with a stress fracture in my foot. My leg was bandaged up and I was given a stick. It was not an auspicious start.

For a month we lived in bed and breakfast accommodation, travelling back and forth to Cambridge at weekends. We had to wait for the mortgage to come through for our buyers in Bar Hill and, as I was unable to drive because of my foot, Ian did all the driving. We had hoped to move at the end of August but there were all sorts of lending restrictions that had to be overcome. Building societies were not allowed by the government to lend more than £25,000 and they also restricted borrowing to two and a half times one income plus a second income, if there was one. We needed more than that if we were to be able to afford the property we wanted to buy. However, banks had more autonomy and, although they normally only lent up to half of a second income, I strategically went on my own to visit our bank manager, at the edge of the market square in Cambridge. I explained that I had secured a tenured lectureship at The University of Bristol that was on an incremental sliding scale. This pressed all the right buttons. The bank manager did not enquire about my husband, who held a temporary position in Cambridge, and was still looking for something closer to Bristol. I did explain that our salaries would be almost equal and found that he was happy to lend us up to two and a half times our joint income, which was more than we needed. With a mortgage of £29,000 and an interest rate of 15%, we would be spending half our income on our house. It was a big commitment.

Ian had completed his doctorate in 1980 and taken a position in the computer labs where he maintained the input-output system to the IBM 370, that was still in use. The code needed to be very efficient and was written in assembler. I recall it being about thirty feet long when printed out, longer than our living room, though I cannot recall why Ian had brought it home. We thought we might commute between Bristol and Cambridge for a while but, again with the help of the grapevine, Ian was offered a position at the University of Bath to act as one of two support officers for anyone in the university with a microcomputer. Adrian Bowyer was deemed to be the hardware specialist and Ian was the software specialist but he was soon issued with a screwdriver and soldering iron as both of them needed to be able to solve any problems that arose

We did not manage to move into our new house until two days before lectures started. We emptied our house in Bar Hill one day and the furniture and books were driven to Bristol to be unloaded the following day. It meant that I was not around for the arrival of new students but I had left instructions for them to meet me for tutorials the next week. On the day we moved in I did briefly pop into the department, dressed in some tatty old clothes, in order to collect some spare curtains that one of my colleagues had lent to us. It was unfortunate that an enterprising first year had located my office. He must have thought I was the cleaning lady when he asked me in enquiring tones, 'Could you tell me where I can find Dr Holyer?' I fear it got us off to a bad start as I replied in stentorian tones, 'I am Dr Holyer!' He was a quiet lad from Port Talbot, not far from by own home in Swansea, and he was looking for reassurance which was not supplied by my intimidating response.

I was just twenty-six years old and easily the youngest member of staff. As I entered the room for my first lecture to a class of two hundred first year physicist and chemists, I comforted myself with the thought that this was their first lecture too. I decided that the stress fracture in my foot would be fine without the stick as I could just about manage without it. I kept my nerves under control by registering that they would not know how university lectures should be conducted. It was quite a hard class to teach as some of the students were very able with top grades in both maths and further maths while other had just scraped the required grade C maths A-level and had been hoping never to have to look at an equation again. It was not unusual for students to complain that they had come to university to read physics and they should not have to do all this maths. They had obviously not heard the quote of Roger Bacon in the thirteenth century who had said that mathematics is the gate and key of the sciences. I was just teaching basic mathematical methods that would be needed later in their degrees and most came to appreciate my lectures in the long run. I settled in to the rhythm of my new life.

In the end Ian only spent eighteen months in Bath as a vacancy arose in the computer science group at Bristol. This was still part of the School of Mathematics. With both of us in the department I was dismayed when my colleagues suggested I should revert to my maiden name so that there were not two Dr Holyers. Most internal communication used initials and I often had difficulty distinguishing between AAW, AJW, EJW and other similar sets of initials. It did not cause Ian or me problems that we had the same surname, though on one occasion it did embarrass a student. He arrived at Ian's office and said that he had missed a few of his lectures and needed the problem sheets that had been handed out. This sort of request happened regularly and Ian asked which course it was. With the response of electromagnetic theory, all became clear. Ian suggested he had not been to any of the lectures as he would have been aware that the lecturer was female. The student was considerably less embarrassed than one might have expected. When he arrived at my office, I gave him what was needed to catch up and he did promise to come to the rest of the lectures.

Ian kept up with his former colleagues in Bath and when they designed and built a new computer, based on a new Motorola 68000 16-bit chip, Ian was asked to help with the software. Designated as a microcomputer, Ian was given the prototype to work on. It was the size of a full size filing cabinet with a wire-wrapped motherboard and it was definitely not portable. I do not know how it acquired its name, the Dark Star, but I sometimes felt it was large enough to generate its own gravitational field. Ian's contribution was to write the backend to the Fortran compiler, which provided the interface between those parts of the language which were machine dependent and standard Fortran. Despite the fact that I was still programming in Fortran, I never used the Dark Star. It did not possess the memory or speed that my fluid dynamics programs needed. I used the university's Honeywell Bull mainframe that was located in the basement of the maths department and got to grips with its Multics time-sharing operating system. Ian's compiler was a success and, in lieu of payment, Ian was allowed to keep the prototype, which pleased Ian. It was our first home computer, although I was happier when we acquired a BBC micro and I could play the arcade games, Pac-Man and Tetris, when I needed to wind down.

We continued going out to the home of Phil Willis, another Bath colleague of Ian. Every Friday we drove twenty miles to Winsley, beyond Bath, where a group of us met to review board games for a gaming magazine. It was a good break from more serious work. One of the games was marketed as the opportunity to play dice with the universe and moved between the large scales of galaxies to the small scale of atoms with an alacrity that would have impressed even the likes of Stephen Hawking. It was unfortunate that the game could always be won by the second player, who merely needed to copy the move of the first player. We had great fun with a mathematical version of scrabble. It was probably perfectly suited to children as it was intended to teach simple arithmetic. However, we discovered that brackets could be added freely to equations and that the set contained a lot of zeros. We ended up with many complicated and esoteric ways to express the fact that zero equals zero. The review we wrote suggested that playing it with four people each with a Ph.D. in maths was probably not advisable.

Lecturing was by now an everyday activity. I always carried sticks of chalk in my bag and retain an abiding hatred of chalk dust which seemed to get into everything. There was a rule that when you left a lecture room you always cleaned the board for the incoming lecturer. This did not always happen. I was told that the normal advice when you arrived to find a dirty board was to ask the prettiest girl in the front row to clean it for you. I generally chose the tallest and handsomest man, as the tops of some of the boards were out of my reach. The lecture rooms in the maths department were not large enough for our first year classes and we used larger lecture theatres in physics, chemistry and the medical school. I did once arrive at a lecture theatre to find an anatomical diagram covering half the available boards with a large notice to the side asking for it not to be deleted. I would have apologised if a name or room number had been left because I could see the amount of work that had gone into the drawing. However, I needed all the board space that was available, quite apart from the fact that I was not willing to lecture to a mixed group of eighteen-year-olds with them being distracted by a picture a woman's private parts. I erased it before the students arrived.

I was far closer in age to the students than to the other applied maths staff who were all over forty. Amongst the thirty teaching staff, there was one other female lecturer, Maria Zaturska. I do remember one student saying to me that Dr Banks and Dr Zaturska seemed to be very friendly. Tempting though it was to spread scandal, I did tell him that they were married to each other. At least I had spared myself that problem by insisting on keeping the name I had been using for the previous five years. I had been asked at my interview if I foresaw any difficulties in moving to Bristol and I knew it was a veiled attempt at asking about my husband's plans. I purposely changed the direction of this question and replied that I thought that the students at Bristol would be as good as those at Cambridge. This proved to be almost true. Students who had been rejected by Cambridge were generally not as good as the ones who had applied with Bristol as their first choice and the students at Bristol were less socially mixed than those at Cambridge. There was a preponderance of white, middle-class southerners. I also felt that there was prejudice against ethnic minorities and poorer students. One day, out of curiosity, I asked the four students in one of my tutorial groups what grades they had been asked for to gain admission to Bristol. One had been asked for three As while the others had all been asked for one A and two Bs. When I queried our admissions officer he said that he always gave higher offers to people from schools with poor reputations. No wonder that Bristol was less diverse than Cambridge. The student whose offer caused me concern had come from an inner city comprehensive school in Leicester and was not a white, middle-class southerner. Following excellent results in the first year exams a congratulatory letter was sent out by the Faculty Office to Miss Popat, supposedly the student concerned. The following day a forlorn Nilesh Popat arrived at my office. He was mortified at the letter he had received. I contacted the person who had sent the letter and she said she was sure that Nilesh was a girl's name, notwithstanding the fact that he was blatantly not a girl. Nilesh was a practising Hindu and I had already learnt about Diwali from him when he had asked permission to return home, missing some lectures, during his first term. Now we talked more, partly because I was unsure how he felt about having a female tutor. It is a conversation that has stayed with me because he complimented me by saying that I was a good Hindu because, as a Christian, I was worshipping an incarnation (that is an avatar) of God. He decided to stay with me as his tutor. He just did not like to be referred as a woman, anymore than I liked to be referred to as a man.

There were some changes that I tried to get implemented because of my gender. I had a problem with the student questionnaires that we were required to distribute at the end of any lecture course. Asking if he was audible and legible, I would receive facetious answers to questions on the quality of my lectures. There were suggestions that he had a very high voice and looked strangely effeminate. It was clear to me that the forms needed to be changed but, when it was put to a vote at a department meeting, a majority decided that they were fine as they were. I had to continue to put up with having the pronoun 'he' applied to me. I did enjoy some of the responses in the questionnaires. At the end of my first term lecturing, one student wrote, 'Dr Holyer should teach Dr Walker how to lecture.' This was very satisfying as Dr Walker had been lecturing for twenty years or so yet it appeared that his lectures were boring, which, knowing him, did not really surprise me. Another student wrote, 'Calculus may be the be all and end all of Dr Holyer's life but it is not the be all and end all of mine.' I might have overdone the enthusiasm. While some of the men in the department thought that I was a feminist, I knew I was not. I wanted everyone to be respected, not just women.

I did not feel supported as a member of staff at Bristol. It seemed as if they wanted to take all my abilities and suck them out of me until I was empty. It may not have been because I was a woman but because I was young. It was just as likely to be women making my life difficult as men. There was a group trying hard to get at least one woman on every committee in the university. I was against this as I did not want to spend all my time on committees. It was a strange idea of equality with nothing about working to people's strengths. There was an assumption that all men were bad and out to get women. This was never my experience. No gender has a monopoly on kindness, caring or power games.

We had known before we moved to Bristol that Ian's mother was terminally ill with breast cancer. Diagnosed in November 1980, she had a course of chemotherapy which, by Christmas, left her frail and weak; barely able to walk at all. However, with regular blood transfusions she regained her strength and, in February 1982, visited us in Bristol. She almost tired us out as we visited the SS Great Britain, docked in Bristol harbour, and travelled to the Roman Baths in nearby Bath. I was very fond of my mother-in-law, who was a big improvement on my own mother. She never criticised me or the way we lived. As 1982 progressed, the blood transfusions became less effective and in May we had a call from Ian's father to tell us she had been taken to Addenbrookes Hospital in Cambridge and were told she did not have long. That weekend we travelled up to see her and found her comatose. As we left the hospital with Ian's father, I had to rapidly turn off the radio in our car as I realised it was playing Chopin's funeral march. It felt surreal. We had to return to Bristol, knowing that we would soon hear bad news. She died a few days later and I was told, by Dr Johnny Walker, who was in charge of such things, that it was not allowed to have time off for the funerals of in-laws. The funeral coincided with exams and fell upon the first day when I was supposed to be invigilating. Fortunately it was not just me who thought Dr Walker was being unreasonable and Bill Boyd offered to do my invigilation. I just hoped there were not any mistakes on the paper that would require my presence. The funeral took place in the Catholic Church in Ely and was a full requiem mass. In those days I did not cry but I still miss Ian's mother who died just before her fifty-ninth birthday.

There were always two invigilators in exams, just in case one needed to leave for any reason, which was most often to accompany someone to the lavatories. At the first exam I did invigilate in Bristol we were very glad that there were two of us. One of the students was sick over his exam paper. I was left in the room to sort things out while the other invigilator, Philip Drazin, accompanied the distressed young man outside to clean himself up. Fortunately the exam was in a lab with taps so I managed to wash off the papers and move the students who had been sitting nearby away from the lingering smell. It was not a paper that I had to mark myself and we decided not to tell the pure maths professor, John Marstrand, who was marking it why it looked as if it had been in a rainstorm. He would probably have refused to mark it. I had plenty of marking of my own and the time scales to complete it were short. I spent days on end hunched over papers, giving myself regular incentives of a cup of coffee or a sweet but the marking required my full attention which stopped me wallowing in grief at my mother-in-law's death.

I tried hard to find the support that I needed in Bristol. When we had first arrived we went to the Anglican chaplaincy church of St Paul's in Clifton. With a robed choir of university students, who looked disengaged from the services, and a more formal liturgy than we were used to, it was not for us. The Anglican chaplain, Melvyn Matthews, wanted to educate staff in theology. I did not need more academic input. We did want to go to a church with some sort of university connection and finally started to go to Tyndale Baptist Church, where the minister, a different Peter Webb to the one I had known at Girton, was part of the chaplaincy team. I appreciated conversations him and with Derek Parsons, who was both a member of Tyndale and a lecturer in the physics department. He understood the pressures of university life. When I said that I felt I had to watch out for knives in my back, he suggested that academics covertly carried stilettos (that is daggers – not shoes!) The politics of life at Bristol University was not for the faint-hearted. We transferred our membership to Tyndale from the ecumenical church in Bar Hill and Ian managed to move from being a Roman Catholic to a Baptist via two handshakes.

My time in Bristol was soon marked by two more family deaths. My mother had a twin brother, Tom, who worked in electronics. He lived in Woking but was commuting twice a week to the Isle of Wight as a consultant to a project to rebuild the airport in Stanley after its destruction in the Falklands War of 1982. As an obese smoker who liked more that the odd pint, he was not in the best of health but it was, nevertheless, a big shock when he had a stroke at the age of fifty-eight and died in November 1982. I had learnt from the death of Ian's mother and did not ask for permission for time off for his funeral. I simply rescheduled my lectures and went. I am not sure that my mother ever really recovered from the shock of his death. She had previously had a heart attack when she was fifty-three and had come close to death herself. I had not then heard about near-death experiences, and neither had she, but she spoke of drifting off down a tunnel with a beautiful garden at the end. When she heard someone say, 'I think she's gone,' she revived and slowly recovered in intensive care. After her brother's death she started to suffer from severe angina and on the day of the first anniversary of his funeral, Friday 25th November 1983, she had a second heart attack, from which she did not recover. Apparently that day she had told my father that she thought Tom wanted her to be with him. I do not know what I make of that. I do know that I had been to the doctor that day and, having rushed from a lecture through a rainstorm to the appointment, arrived on time only to be kept waiting for over an hour. I was told that my blood pressure was too high and that I would have to go on pills for blood pressure for the rest of my life. I rang my mother to talk about it and two hours later my father rang to say she had just been taken to hospital and was pronounced dead on arrival. For years I felt as if I had killed her by worrying her about my health. In fact, I did not have high blood pressure at all. It was just a single anomalous measurement caused by the rush to get to the appointment followed by the waiting. The doctor remained adamant that I must have high blood pressure because I was overweight, despite subsequent normal measurements. She told me that I was in denial and was not willing to consider the possibility that she might be wrong. It took me a year but eventually I changed to a male doctor who checked everything out and gave me a clean bill of health with normal blood pressure. I decided that above all else I wanted a competent doctor and gender is irrelevant.

My father remarried on June 15th 1985. Our family silver cabinet contained a silver-plated tea service, never used, inscribed with the date in 1885 that his parents had married. It seemed quite a coincidence when we realised my father was remarrying on the centenary of his parents' marriage. Isabel Mitchell was a member of the same Methodist church as my parents. Her husband, Dennis, had died from cancer six months before my mother and, like my father, she was lonely. Their courtship started with my father going round to her house in the evening to watch television and then they spent a holiday in Spain, staying with Isabel's brother and sister-in-law, George and Norma Hinds. At Christmas, a year after my mother's death, my father came to stay with us and, after he had gone home, I noticed, from our itemised phone bill, that he had been calling Isabel daily. I was not surprised when he told me that they were planning to marry. My father had not been in good health since before his retirement in 1981. He was suffering from pain and loss of sensation caused by a cyst in his neck and had had surgery six months before my mother's death. Following her death we had seen him almost every weekend, mostly in Swansea, but sometimes he drove to see us in Bristol. It was an enormous time commitment. From a practical (and somewhat callous) point of view his marriage took a lot of pressure off me. Isabel had always wanted children so I hoped that I would be able to have a good relationship with her. Unfortunately it was young children who delighted her and we never had the close relationship that I would have liked. Her black-and-white world-view was too different from my own but I remain profoundly grateful to her for the care she gave to my father in his final years.

Historically most computer science departments grew out of mathematics departments. It slowly became clear in Bristol that computer science needed to be a department in its own right and to move from the Science Faculty to Engineering, where it could make links with the electrical engineering department. There seemed to be quite a lot of inertia when it came to putting this change into practice. A meeting of all the academic staff in the School of Mathematics held in 1984 was dithering over making a final decision. I found myself getting impatient and suggested that it was clear that mathematicians and computer scientists could not happily live together and it was time to formally split. The decision was made and the new department of computer science was created. Only Ian, who had been sitting next to me at that meeting, noticed the irony with which I had spoken. Fortunately my words did not have the same effect on our marriage.

I used to say that a university lectureship is one half teaching, one half administration and one half research. There was certainly more to fit in than time available but the Easter and summer breaks were normally a good time to catch up on research. They were not vacations for the academic staff but they did give a breathing space. During term we had a weekly research seminar but, apart from that, it was impossible to get a long enough span of time to get anything serious done. I did regularly review articles for the Journal of Fluid Mechanics but never once managed to get one done in usual working hours. I kept up research contacts, both in the UK and around the world, which meant that I could get to conferences and arrange research visits with colleagues for the vacations, provided that I was prepared to engage with the onerous task of applying for research grants. There has never been a large group of people working on double-diffusion and an international conference for thirty or so recognised scientists who worked in the area was arranged to take place at Santa Barbara, California in March 1983, sponsored by NOAA, who had previously supported my summer fellowship at Woods Hole. It took place before the end of term and I had to squeeze my lectures on electromagnetic theory into eight weeks, rather than the usual ten, but I was determined to get there, despite a bout of flu and my father having spinal surgery a few weeks earlier. March in California, at a hotel overlooking the Pacific Ocean was a pleasant change from Bristol and my lingering cough soon disappeared in the spring sun, as I watched humming birds supping on nectar. I gave a paper on interleaving which was well-received and it was good to be able to chat with others around the pool about their research. I met quite a few people for the first time, including Ann Gargett, an oceanographer from the Canadian government labs on Vancouver Island. She was the only other woman at the conference but, as a whole, I felt as if I had found a group to which I belonged. Largely Australian, American and British, we got on as friends as well as colleagues. Some areas of academic research are rife with in-fighting but we would work together to solve problems, freely sharing results, with the knowledge that credit would always be given where credit was due.

As I had needed to apply for a travel grant to get to the conference in Santa Barbara, I decided to lengthen the trip to five weeks, travelling up the west coast of the U.S., returning to Bristol just in time for the summer term. On leaving Santa Barbara, I flew down to San Diego, where I visited Scripps Institute, set up by Walter Munk, who had left Austria at the Anschluss of WWII and had worked on forecasts in preparation for D-Day. He invited me to his home in La Jolla, following the seminar I had given and I met his wife, Judith, who was very keen on drama. They had a small amphitheatre by the ocean in their large garden, reminding me of our honeymoon visit to the Minack theatre in Cornwall. Three years later I was surprised to bump into Walter in the ladies lavatory in the Engineering Department in Cambridge. His wife had suffered from polio as a child and was confined to a wheelchair. She needed help to get to the toilet and he told me that he had learnt that it worked better taking her into the ladies than the gents. I had just been to a lecture that was part of the G.I. Taylor centenary conference, at which we had been told that G.I. Taylor liked to conduct fluids experiments in the gents toilet, and was feeling aggrieved that this excluded women. There were only two women in tenured university positions attending that conference out of two hundred people in total, myself and Ruby Krishnamurti, who I would have to describe as an American originally from India, in case I gave the wrong idea by describing her as an American Indian. It made me laugh to find Walter in the ladies and I realised that I had no need to feel excluded.

My trip in 1983 continued with me flying back to Los Angeles and hiring a car to drive up to San Francisco. Stopping off in Monterey I visited the Naval Postgraduate School where I met Tom Osborne. The students there were largely male naval officers in crisp uniforms, although most of the academic staff were civilians who were given the status of officers so that they could eat in the officers' mess. This was not an environment where I was comfortable but I was glad to be shown around the area by Tom. Carmel, home of Clint Eastwood, was not far off and we took the seventeen mile drive around the coast. I travelled on to San Francisco and took a break to visit the Napa valley vineyards, tasting white port for the first time. As I drove back into the city along a steep and windy road down to the Golden Gate Bridge, the driver of the car that had been following me pulled up alongside at some traffic lights and informed me, in no uncertain terms, that my brake lights were not working. I was not surprised that he was frustrated but he had avoided going into the back of me. The following day I flew up to Seattle. At the airport I was approached and asked to sign a petition in favour of peace, which sounded fine until I realised it was actually supporting the 'Star Wars' strategic defence initiative of Ronald Reagan to put a weaponised defensive shield into space. I did not sign and continued to Seattle where I spoke at the University of Washington. Mike Howe, an oceanographer there, was involved in the SALT (Strategic Arms Limitation) talks that were then underway. I preferred his approach as a way to seek peace; mutual respect and accountability rather than 'mad' (mutually assured destruction) alternatives. From Seattle I flew up to Vancouver and also visited Victoria on Vancouver Island. The weather had deteriorated as I moved up the coast and it was snowing in Vancouver when I was there. I flew home after five weeks of solitary travel, glad to see Ian again. It had been a lovely way to spend the Easter vacation and I was full of new research ideas.

I am not sure how I got talking to Mike Proctor about the planform of salt fingers, known to be square. I think it was at the pool in Santa Barbara. He had a technique to study the evolution of instabilities using nonlinear methods and was looking for problems that he could use it on. He came to see me in Bristol and a few months later I went to Cambridge, where he arranged for me to stay in the judge's suite at Trinity College. I slept in a most uncomfortable bed, rumoured to have been slept in by both Queen

Victoria and Prince Albert, in an enormous room. I had the thought that the mattress had not been changed since. A maid arrived early in the morning, drew back the curtains and asked me what I would like for breakfast. It was like life from a lost era. However Mike and I completed our work and sent it off for publication.

I spent the summer of 1984 at the University of British Columbia in Vancouver, working with Larry Mysak, an oceanographer interested in wave problems. Ian had managed to arrange to work with Ernie Cockayne, a friend of Belá Bollobás, in Victoria on Vancouver Island. We rented a condominium in West Vancouver where we spent most weekends. Ian travelled back and forth on a scenic ferry route that ran past islands and through Active Passage. I enjoyed life in Vancouver where the oceanography department arranged several beach barbecues at which we baked Alaskan salmon in a hollow in the sand. Each day I ate lunch at the Staff club on a balcony overlooking the sea. They had a cashless system; sending out monthly bills. We were identified by signing with the first four letters of our surnames, so all summer I was, to my amusement, known as HOLY. I worked hard, solving a problem that Larry had not known how to attack, and showed how Rossby waves, propagating across the Pacific ocean can generate trench waves down the western coasts of Canada and America. I acquired an Erdös number of three that summer, by writing up the work on trench waves with Larry Mysak. Erdös was a prolific Hungarian graph theorist who collaborated with many other mathematicians and measuring your Erdös number is a standard hobby for pure mathematicians. While wandering around Vancouver we saw adverts for cruises up the Inside Passage to Alaska. Thinking it was a once in a lifetime opportunity, we joined a Holland America ship at the beginning of September for the cruise up to Glacier Bay. With just five of us on board who were not US or Canadian citizens, we had to get up at an unearthly hour to clear customs and immigration when we arrived at the first port. At the end of the trip our U.S. entry permits were not collected from our passports which caused me difficulty the next time I needed a U.S. visa, as I had to prove I had not become an illegal immigrant. In Alaska, autumn was approaching and we saw salmon leaping upstream to spawn as well as hearing glaciers calving into the sea. We watched the ice that had been hauled on board being carved into dolphins and fish for display at meals. At the final banquet of our cruise, we enjoyed the ice-cream dessert of baked Alaska that was paraded into the dining room by the chefs. We assumed that this was done because we were in Alaska, little knowing that it is a feature of all tourist cruises around the world. As we left the ship, back in Vancouver, we saw the board of photos that had been put up to give a flavour of the trip to the next set of passengers. Ian and I were surprised to notice that we featured in almost half the pictures. Then I realised that we were less than half the age of most of the other passengers. Now that we are older ourselves, we have returned to cruising, with its leisurely pace of life, and plan to repeat the Alaskan cruise some day.

Back in Bristol life felt like a rat race, where the rats had won. I took on some masters students and a Ph.D. student, which gave me an outlet for some of my research ideas, but there was no time to do any research of my own. By 1986 I was feeling ground down by overwork. It was not that the work itself was hard. I could do it with my hands tied behind my back. It was just that there was too much of it and I was too much of a perfectionist not to do everything to the best of my ability. Each morning I arrived at the department with a sinking feeling. I was having to spend the most time on the things that I least enjoyed. I had made the mistake of asking if it might be possible to get a terminal in my office, with the result that I was asked to put in a bid to the university. I effectively became the departmental computer officer, without any time allocation for the work. Every day I had to deal with problems. I had managed to get money for the department, so that we could link up two BBC microcomputers as terminals to the university-owned Honeywell mainframe. I had intended it for my benefit, so that I could keep up my research work without having to waste time going down to the basement terminals, but I found it just gave me more work. The terminals lived on trolleys on the third and fourth floors of the department and staff could book them and wheel them into their offices whenever they wanted to use them. I was required to provide the maintenance and support. Several of us had gone in one weekend to install an Ethernet network around the offices, pulling cables through the walls, installing the router in the conveniently-placed office of Professor Drazin. As more computers were bought I had to put in word-processing chips, ensuring that the twenty-eight or so pins on the long chips did not bend or break as they were inserted into the motherboard. Everyday I had to deal with issues from people who could not get their terminals working. My first response was always to ask if the RS232 was plugged in upside down. It could be inserted either way and I had marked them all. It gave no error message if upside down and simply failed to connect. When the Honeywell computer was coming up for replacement a committee was formed to advise the university on the requirements for a replacement and a mathematician, a physicist, a chemist and a biochemist were appointed. I found myself on that committee. All the members were major computer users and it is the only university committee that I have ever been on that had a balance of genders, as the biochemist was also female. The university was starting to introduce word-processing equipment and offered the department some Rank Xerox word-processing machines. Unfortunately they were of no use to us as they did not have a facility for adding mathematical symbols or equations. I joined a couple of staff from the computer centre to source something that might work for mathematicians and for our departmental secretaries. We really wanted something that was WYSIWYG, pronounced whizzy wig. I am never sure about acronyms and it might have been easier to say, 'What you see is what you get.' We found a company in nearby Melksham that was marketing a system called 'Triad Technical Typing' or 'T3' and it fulfilled the needs of the department for a few years. One of the secretaries, Rhoda, was especially expert in its use and later moved on to using LaTeX which is more like a programming language. I kept up with all my lectures and the marking that they generated. I was always inclined to say yes whenever I was asked to take something on. When asked to become chair of the university computer users' committee, I prevaricated. I did not want the job as I could see it would move me away from the research that I enjoyed. I decided that it was time to organise a sabbatical year away from Bristol, even though I would have to arrange for my own funding.

At the time I often suffered from what I used to call terminal backache. The chairs and trolleys that the terminals were on did not give a good ergonomic position. There was no space under the trolley for your legs so it was a long reach to the keyboard. Perhaps overwork also played a part. It seems to me that the more I did the more I was taken advantage of. I feel someone should have noticed but, if I ever made any sort of comment, I was told that it was traditional that junior staff worked harder than those who were more senior. I empathised enormously with a student who decided to have a year out after her degree. She said to me, 'Stop the world. I want to get off.' I needed a break too.

It is only in looking back that I realise how much I was overworking and how stressed I had become. My top priority in life was work, followed by my family and then God. It took a trip to the other side of the world to turn everything upside down.

9. Life Turned Upside Down

I got in touch with Trevor McDougall, who was working at the Australian Government oceanographic research labs in Hobart, Tasmania. I had first met Trevor at DAMTP, where he had been a Ph.D. student a couple of years ahead of me, and we had become reacquainted at the conference in Santa Barbara. I was very pleased to receive a grant for travel and research from the Science Research Council, despite the fact that I was told that there was not a chance I would get it when I applied. I worked on the principle that if you do not ask, you do not get. I think it was the reference from Sir James Lighthill that worked the magic. It meant that I could start to organise the sabbatical, without needing any financial support from Bristol. The oceanographic labs were part of the Commonwealth Scientific and Industrial Research Organisation, more commonly known as the CSIRO, and had moved a few years earlier to Hobart from Cronulla on the coast near Sydney, to the disappointment of some staff. Tasmania tends to be regarded as backward compared to the avant-garde world of Sydney but the relocation was enforced by the government as part of a plan to reinvigorate the economy of Tasmania, rather like the British government opening the DVLC in South Wales. The new fisheries division and oceanographic labs were set at the edge of the harbour in Hobart with a dock for the research vessel, Franklin, named after a nineteenth-century polar explorer. Fortunately there had never been a public vote as to how the Franklin should be named so there had been no similar

147

controversy to that provoked when Boaty McBoatface came out as the popular choice for the equivalent British research vessel. On my arrival, I was allocated part of an office, sharing with an academic visitor from mainland China, overlooking the harbour where I could admire the seals swimming around outside and watch the passing ships.

Trevor McDougall had completed his Ph.D. on turbulence in the basement lab at DAMTP, where he had needed to work at dead of night, in order to avoid disruption to his laser measuring equipment, caused by the lorries passing in Silver Street. I now hoped to be able to do some work with him where we could integrate theory and experiment. He was running a lab, as well as making measurements in the ocean, using a device called a Bunyip, which measured the fine structure of temperature and salinity. I was always interested in the relationship between theory and experiment, which could each be used to enhance the other. Using a long tank we planned to look at the processes that occur when two water masses with the same density stratification but differing temperature and salinity met. I hoped to do some experiments with him. That may sound bad, though probably not quite as bad as the sign we used to put on the door that said, 'Keep Out! Experiments in progress in the dark.' I do wonder what people passing imagined we were up to!

I arranged to spend the entire academic year from September 1986 until August 1987 in Australia, with six months in Hobart, three months in Sydney at the maths department of the University of New South Wales and three months at the Research School of Earth Sciences at the Australian National University in Canberra. I would have gone alone but was pleased when Ian also managed to arrange a year's leave from the department and we set off, travelling via Vancouver and Fiji.

I found a much better balance between work and the rest of life in Australia. Something like fifty people worked at the CSIRO Division of Oceanography in Hobart and all the work was led by the research scientists. I became part of their group and, although the only woman, felt more accepted for myself there than I had become used to at Bristol. The banter was friendly and I could give as good as I got. Every Friday after work there was a visit to The Custom House, the local pub, and, although I have never been a follower of cricket, could provoke a lively conversation by simply asking who was winning. I gathered that 1986 was a good year for English cricket. Ian and I bought a cheap car and at weekends travelled around Tasmania, visiting the rainforest and beaches, as well as the penal colony at Port Arthur, which had an eerie feeling to it. On Sundays we generally went with Trevor and his family to Lenah Valley Baptist Church, where we found a friendly welcome from the minister, Malcolm Eberhard, and the rest of the congregation. This stood us in good stead later when I became ill, as Ian and I were provided with many casseroles to keep our stamina up.

Early on in my time in Hobart there was a conference on ocean mixing. I gave a seminar at that meeting which was recorded. Unusually, I heard my own voice and was surprised by how plummy I sounded. I like to think it was the effect of being surrounded by so many Australian accents, but fear my Oxbridge education had got the better of me. I do find it strange that whenever I try to mimic an accent, be it Australian, American or Indian, it always comes out with a Welsh lilt. Perhaps it is best to just stick with my accent as it is and accept myself as I am. One of the invited speakers at that conference was Roger Revelle, an American climatographer, who presented data showing the link between carbon dioxide levels and global temperature rises. This was the scientist who inspired the presidential candidate, Al Gore, to make the film 'An Inconvenient Truth', which helped to bring the problem of the human impact on the environment to public and political consciousness. I found myself registering the problem that sea level rises could cause in poor, low-level countries like Bangladesh, where they would not be able to afford expensive sea defences. Simple thermal expansion of water causes a sea level rise of one meter for each degree rise in temperature and almost all of Bangladesh is less than one meter above sea level. It surprises me that there are still people who deny climate change and, even more, that they include Christopher Monckton, who was at college with me.

Christmas came and, despite the soaring temperatures, Santas in fur-trimmed suits were often seen out on the streets with reindeer and snowmen stationed nearby. We enjoyed listening to the Salvation Army band playing carols at the harbourside, although singing 'In the bleak midwinter' at nine o'clock in the evening, as the sun shone down upon us, did leave me feeling slightly bemused. We discovered that almost all Australians have a hot Christmas lunch with both turkey and gammon joints as well as all the trimmings, of pigs in blankets, sprouts, parsnips, stuffing, cranberry sauce and bread sauce, all followed by Christmas pudding, whether they live in one of the metropolitan cities or in the middle of the outback. Apparently, it is only foreigners who have a barbie on the beach.

I can lay claim to having gone swimming in the sea on New Year's Day, although it is not a great accomplishment in the warmth of an Australian summer. We went to seven-mile beach, just outside Hobart, with a picnic and spent the day in the shade of the eucalyptus trees, watching the children playing cricket on the beach, and occasionally cooling off in the sea. It has become the spot that I return to in my mind whenever I need to find a place of stillness. That day we continued our Australian experience by going to the cinema to see the recently released film, 'Crocodile Dundee', which portrayed a different life to that which we found in Hobart. We had already discovered that Australian jokes frequently portrayed Tasmanians as backward. Hobart has some of the oldest buildings in Australia and many of the locals take pride in being able to trace their lineage back to convicts transported from the UK, often for minor misdemeanours. With balconies of iron lace, Hobart reminded me of England as it must have been in Victorian times. We were often mistaken for locals as strong British accents like ours were not uncommon. In fact, Ian had nearly been brought up in Hobart. When Ian's parents were first married, they had considered moving to Australia as Ten Pound Poms, under a scheme where the government paid the boat fare in order to gain immigrants. Ian's father had managed to obtain a job in Hobart and the date for them to move had been set but Ian's mother had become pregnant. She was not allowed to travel, presumably because the authorities were worried about any possible complications of childbirth, and they were told they could not reapply until the baby reached its first birthday. So Ian was born in Aylesbury, Buckinghamshire, rather than Hobart, Tasmania, and grew up British. Still with a wanderlust and a desire to live somewhere warmer, Ian's father took the opportunity to work as a general factotum at the Royal Air force airbase in Cyprus, where Ian grew up delighting in swimming and snorkelling in the warm Mediterranean sea. They returned to the UK in 1961 and Ian got used to cooler weather. He decided that swimming in the cold British waters was not for him and can no longer be persuaded to go swimming at all. Ian's parents gave up their plans to emigrate and settled in Bushey, Hertfordshire, not far from me in Hemel Hempstead, where Ian's brother and sister were both born. It was only when we told Ian's father that we were going to Hobart that Ian heard this story. Ian's father was envious of us, travelling to a place where he had once aspired to live. I do not often play the game of 'What if', but it did occur to me that if Ian's parents had emigrated to Hobart in the 1950s we might still have met and got married.

The heights of sophistication come to Hobart each year with the arrival of the racing yachts from the Sydney-Hobart boat race that takes place between Christmas and New Year. I have never been to Monaco, but I imagine it as Hobart was that week, with ostentatious wealth being flaunted. The CSIRO had entered a yacht in the race and used satellite data to predict the wind and the East Australia Current. Aiming to do well with its scientific approach, it took a substantially different route to most of the other boats. It did not come in last, but it was not clear that it had gained any advantage from its unusual route. The crew included the Chief of the Division of Oceanography, Angus McEwan, and on his arrival into Hobart he was less than his usual dapper self, with a week's beard-growth and a haunted look that showed he was seriously short of sleep.

In the middle of January I had hoped to go on a trip on the Franklin with Trevor to trial the Bunyip but I would have been going to observe rather than to help. The plan was that I would take the final berth. However new employees at the CSIRO were required to be able to work at sea and the berth that I was to have occupied was needed to test out a new member of staff. I was not all that upset. I was not sure that I wanted to find out how sea-sick I would get on a small ocean-going research vessel.

It was probably just as well that I did not go to sea that week as I might have needed surgery on board. The trip was the last one sailing from Hobart for a couple of years as the Franklin was about to be relocated in Perth to work off Western Australia. Before it set off, there was a party on the dockside to mark both its return from the week's trip and its departure for Perth. Celebrating with champagne and rich fruit cake, I was not very surprised when, the following morning, I woke up with stomachache. I went in to work, hoping that distraction would help, but I felt no better and our lab technician advised me to go home and take some milk of magnesia. I took his advice but was feeling worse by the evening. We decided it was time to call a doctor and Ian looked through the Yellow Pages to find one that was local and willing to pay a house call. By then I was curled up on the bed and not at all keen to move.

The doctor arrived overdressed in a dinner suit as he was just on his way out to what must have been a formal dinner. He rapidly diagnosed appendicitis and a need for immediate surgery. I was stunned. I had never before felt the need to ask for a house call from a doctor and now I was about to be sent to hospital. I had not been to hospital since I was born. There was no reciprocal arrangement between the NHS and Medicare in Australia so it was fortunate that we had taken out medical insurance. Ian drove me to St John's Hospital, a private hospital near the Cascade brewery on the outskirts of Hobart. I was operated on at 11.30pm at night.

When I came to after the surgery I was completely disorientated. I could see but was utterly unable to move a muscle. I heard someone ask if the anaesthetist was still there. They said they could not wake me up. I tried to let them know that I was awake but failed.

I am uncertain what happened next but I came to when I was transferred back to the bed in the ward. As I tried to sleep my arms were continually pulled out from under the sheets so that my blood pressure could be monitored. I left my appendix in Hobart, Tasmania. It does not have the same ring or romanticism as the phrase, 'I left my heart in San Francisco.' I do hope it has been disposed of. The surgeon came to see me the next day and said he was very glad that he had operated so late at night as the appendix would almost certainly have burst by morning.

I returned home to our flat a week later. I was not recovering well. I had spent the week in hospital regularly fainting. The nurses were less than sympathetic and said I was just being neurotic, complaining at having to help me up from the floor, as if I had done it on purpose. I had never fainted before and have never fainted since and my suspicion is that it was a lingering effect of the anaesthetic. I discovered that the CSIRO was most well-known in the Hobart community for a murder that had been committed by one of the academic staff. The lady in the next bed informed me that she lived in Midway Point, close to the Hobart sewage works, where evidence of the gruesome murder was found. One of the nurses asked where I worked and when I responded, 'The CSIRO labs', she asked if that was where Rory Thompson had worked. Responding in the affirmative, she continued by telling me that he had fabricated his scientific results as well as murdering his wife. I knew this was not true as I had been studying some of his work on the East Australia Current, with a view to following it up. I told her that she was wrong and that there were people who could prove it but did not mention that I was one of them. Rory Thompson had been found guilty but insane and was detained at Her Majesty's Pleasure at the local prison. Everything was churning around inside me and my thoughts seemed to be going faster and faster, like a parallel processor in a computer. I asked myself, 'Am I insane, like Rory?'

After three days at home, Ian was not coping. I wanted to help him but doing the cleaning at 3am just kept him awake. The doctor, who had first visited and diagnosed the appendicitis, lived just around the corner from us and was visiting twice a day. His name was Rob Walters and it is not an exaggeration to say that he saved my life. He arranged for me to be readmitted to a different private hospital, St Helen's, in the city centre, in a GP bed where I was under his care.

This was where my life truly turned upside down; on Sunday 1st February, 1987. It has been the defining experience of my life. I had been moved into a room on my own. I think I must have been disrupting other patients. When I had arrived at the hospital I had been offered a TV at $10 per day, which I had declined. That morning I saw a set outside my room and wheeled it in. After watching the Sunday morning cartoons, a service came on from a Baptist Church in Adelaide. As I watched and listened I had a tremendous sense of the presence of God with me. This was not my usual experience and I feared it was simply a sign of my complete insanity. The service was one of adult baptism by total immersion and when it came to communion I ate biscuits and grapes in order to participate. As the service ended with the words from Matthew's gospel, 'Lo, I am with you always, to the end of time', the experience of God with me continued. Indeed, it is still continuing. I realised that I wanted to be baptised by total immersion. I was very confused. I had been baptised, with a tiny amount of water, when I was twenty-one. Why did I think that I needed to be baptised again, eleven years later?

Later that day I was moved back to the room to which I had first been admitted, sharing with a lady who was recovering from a hysterectomy. The bed was very high and, with the open wound from my recent surgery, it was extremely hard to get in or out. When I was in it I was afraid that I might fall out of such a narrow bed. I first attempted to get the mattress onto the floor and, when that was stopped, I tried to sleep on the floor. The nurses got very cross with me. I locked myself in the lavatory, curled up into a foetal ball, fearing that I was completely mad. When Rob Walters arrived he was furious with the nurses. He assured me that I was not mad. I think he must have been distinguishing mental illness from madness. The following day I was assessed and sent to a private psychiatric unit on the other side of the river, not far from the prison. I was now truly terrified.

I expected to be locked up for the rest of my life, unable to function in the real world. I could not look at my hands, as I thought of Rory Thompson and his dismembered wife. Irrationally, I feared he would escape from prison and come to kill me. My mind was going round really fast, yet I feared I would forget everything. My mind was central to my academic life and my sense of identity and I was losing it. As far as I was concerned the experience that I had on 1st February was the sort of thing that happened to fundamentalist members of the Christian Union. It was not the sort of thing that happened to me.

There was a white board in the common room of the clinic on which the days events were written. One morning, finding it blank, I spontaneously wrote on it, 'Be your own true self.' I have not been able to trace how that idea occurred to me. It feels like it was God-given. It is an aphorism that I now try to live by I had been brought up constantly being told, 'You can't do that. What would people think!', along with, 'Why on earth do you want to do that? You must be mad.' There was no space for me to be me and the tension of trying to keep everybody else happy had finally broken me. I left the psychiatric unit after three weeks with a diagnosis of bipolar affective disorder and a prescription for Largactil, a major tranquilliser.

The televised service from Adelaide had stayed with me. Malcolm Eberhard, our minister in Hobart, was away on holiday, so, guessing an address, I wrote to the minister who had taken the service at Flinders Street Baptist Church, Adelaide. Having sent a letter to a Rev Barry Hibbert in Adelaide, I was surprised to receive a response from London. He had not known the service was being shown again as a repeat and was pleased to hear of the effect it had had on me. He had moved six months earlier to Bloomsbury Baptist Church on Shaftesbury Avenue in London and was now living in Mornington Crescent, close to Regent's Park, where the summer sun of Australia had been replaced by the snow and slush of a cold British winter. I also wrote to Peter Webb, the minister at Tyndale in Bristol. Both Barry and Peter wished me well, as if what had happened was not unusual. I have met Barry Hibbert twice since then. The first time was at Bloomsbury, five years later, when I had applied for a new post as Baptist Chaplain to the University of London. It was strange explaining to the interviewing panel, chaired by Barry Hibbert, how it was that I came to be training as a minister. The second occasion on which we met stranger still. It was just a few years ago and I was in Bath for the annual gathering of British Quakers, which was taking place on the university campus. The Swarthmore lecture that year was given by Ben Pink Dandelion and had transformation as a major theme. As a young man Ben had been an anarchist and had changed his name by deed poll to Pink Dandelion. Travelling across America he had found God on a Greyhound bus. It was not until after he had joined Quakers that he had any experience of Christ and he invited those present to reflect on the experiences of transformation that they had known in their lives. The following day, as I was reflecting, someone I knew called out to me. I was in the Quaker Meeting House in Bath viewing the embroidered Quaker tapestry from Kendal and was surprised to turn to see Gill Collins, who I had known when she was part of a liturgical dance group run by Elizabeth Webb at Tyndale. Gill then introduced me to her husband, Barry Hibbert. Here was an architect of my transformation standing before me. Barry immediately remembered our connection and we chatted for a while. Gill and Barry live most of the year in Australia so it was amazing to just bump into them. I did know that, following the death of his wife and his retirement back to Adelaide, he had married Gill, but was not expecting to meet them. It felt like an affirmation of what had occurred on 1st February 1987. The experience of the presence of God was genuine, even though I had found it so hard to accept at the time.

I was baptised by total immersion on April 10th 1987 at Hobart Baptist Church. I had chosen the hymns. The final hymn was one Ian and I had at our wedding, this time sung to the tune we knew. 'O perfect love, all human thought transcending. Lowly we kneel in prayer before thy throne. That theirs may be the love which knows no ending. Whom though for evermore dost join as one.' I saw baptism as something like marriage. I was becoming the bride of Christ. One of the other hymns I chose was, 'Dear Lord and Father of mankind. Forgive our foolish ways. Re-clothe us in our rightful minds. In purer lives thy service find. In deeper reverence praise.' I knew I was unwell and was in the suicidal depths of depression. I really liked the idea that I might be re-clothed in my rightful mind. The sermon followed a common theme for adult baptism; that of dying with Christ and rising again. Following the service I could not stop crying. It was the first time I had cried since I was four. When I was asked why I was crying I could only reply, 'God loves me.' The depression did not lift yet I knew that I had found something I could rely on and trust. Now it feels to me as if my defences had become so strong that it took the experiences in Australia to break them down. I had a breakdown but it was also a breakthrough into a new life. I would not see it as being born again because my prior life is as important as what has come since. Nevertheless if I were drawing a chart of my life it would appear as a jump; discontinuous and non-differentiable.

I had received an invitation to give a seminar at the University of Western Australia in Perth and, having already had to cancel a trip to the annual Australasian applied maths conference in New Zealand, I was keen to go. The cheapest tickets we could get were called 'Circle Australia' and allowed us five stopovers, as long as one stop was not at a state capital. We decided to go to Brisbane, Sydney, Canberra and Melbourne, as well as Perth, with a break of a few days in Alice Springs so that we could get to see Ayers Rock. I was still not well and had moved on to anti-depressants but the seminar in Perth went well. Visiting the theatre, we saw the Gilbert and Sullivan operetta, 'HMS Pinafore', with Paul Eddington from the British sitcom, 'Yes, Prime minister!' playing the admiral. We arrived at Alice Springs on a Saturday and had a spare day before our trip to Ayers Rock so we decided, on May 12th 1987, to go to a service at John Flynn Memorial Church. Named after the founder of the flying doctor service, this church was part of the Uniting Church in Australia. It was designed for the climate, with walls that did not quite reach the floor, so that there was a through draught in the hot weather and a means to survive occasional flooding. The sermon was based on a text from the gospel of John, 'I have come that you may have life, life in all its fullness.' As I listened an idea entered my head. For a long time I just regarded it as a daft idea but it would not go away. I did not speak of it to any one. How could I possibly become a minister and what did ministry have to do with life in all its fullness anyway?

We continued our trip around Australia, first visiting Ayers Rock, which Ian climbed, while I was driven around the base. It is easy to see how this enormous, isolated boulder, framed on dry, desert evenings by magnificent sunsets, became a place of spiritual significance to the aborigines. Since we were there its name has reverted to its earlier name of Uluru and tourists can no longer climb to the top. After taking over the whole country, it is good to see part of it returned to the aboriginal population. We continued to Brisbane where, after I gave a seminar, we were shown the tower blocks of the Gold Coast. In Sydney, Canberra and Melbourne we mixed academic visits with visits to the tourist sites. I was struck by seeing quintessentially English Morris Dancers outside the Coles department store in the centre of Melbourne and was ready to go home to Bristol.

Ian and I returned to the UK on the day after the general election in June 1987. Our plane broke down in Jakarta and we had an unscheduled twenty-four hour stay in Indonesia. I was still ill; very depressed. I thought we would never get home. We had tenants in our house in Bristol so we spent our first month home staying with my father and Isabel. My father had become increasingly disabled during the year we were away and was now unable to walk at all. It was not easy watching as he struggled to stand but it was good that he had Isabel to look after his daily needs.

While still staying in Swansea we were pleased to be invited to the wedding of our old friend, Dave Lever, who married Ticia in Christchurch, Abingdon. It was the first time I felt vaguely happy after the onset of depression in April. Dave settled in Abingdon, where he and Ticia had three children. Dave became a lay reader in the Anglican church and, now retired from Harwell, he is involved at a church plant of Christchurch in a local estate, Long Furlong. Over the years following Dave and Ticia's marriage, Ian and I quite often went to Christchurch, because my brother and Penny moved very close by and joined the church. Penny took up a lectureship in Engineering at Oxford University and a fellowship at Lady Margaret Hall and also, with the help of a succession of nannies, she and David brought up their four children. David commuted first to Martlesham, near Ipswich, where British Telecom had its research headquarters, and then all around the world when he became European Networking Manager for DEC, the Digital Equipment Corporation, that was a major computer supplier in the 1980s. Their two youngest

[handwritten note:] in LMH register Penny Robert, Fellow in engineering 1988

children were baptised at Christchurch and Penny is still involved there. It is sad that David and Penny's marriage broke down, affected by the stresses of David's travelling and the demands of a young family. Both are now again happily married to other people and their four children seem to have survived; not put off marriage. With a wedding every summer for four years, I now find myself a great aunt eight times over, which does nothing for my fantasy that I am still young.

Returning to Bristol it was clear that I was not fit for work. My GP referred me to a psychiatrist. First I saw a female senior registrar, who was very strong on empathy. She could only see that it must be very hard for me working as a lecturer in an almost entirely male environment. It felt to me as if she saw herself when she looked at me. She assumed that it was my male working environment that was keeping me depressed. When she went on holiday, I saw her consultant, David Cook, and continued to see him. He listened. I could not believe that someone was really willing to listen to me. I think my real problem was that I was not listening to myself. I had spent too long trying to please others. Eventually I told him about my experience on May 12th 1987 in Alice Springs. I hoped it would go away if I did not think about it. It was in talking to David Cook that I first admitted that I sometimes thought about doing something completely different. Unsurprisingly he asked me what I had in mind. When I responded that I had thoughts of becoming a Baptist minister he completely floored me by saying that was what he thought I would say. He was an agnostic, but it was very helpful to me to be able to explore the ideas that I was having with someone who did not tell me what I should, or should not, be doing.

I finally got my nerve up and went to see Rob Ellis, the new minister of Tyndale Baptist Church, in his study at the church. He told me the process by which people could become ministers and I was comforted because there were so many hurdles on the way that I could not envisage that I would ever be accepted. I did discover that in order to become a Baptist minister it was necessary to have been baptised by total immersion. I almost wished I had not been baptised before we had gone to Alice Springs. Then I would have known things were happening in the wrong order and I might have been able to convince myself that I should not proceed. Rob could see the difficulty I was having in working out what to do. He quoted the hymn, 'Lead, kindly light, amid the encircling gloom,' which expressed my position and somewhat consoled me as I realised that Cardinal Newman and others had also felt this way. Our first meeting ended with him telling me to get in touch if I wanted to take the process any further. I only waited three days. I knew I had to continue to 'test the call'. Rob came round to our house and I said, 'Why me?' His response was, 'Why not?' At the time I was concerned that, as Rob is younger than me, he might never before have had a similar conversation with a member of his congregation. I did not know he was already a member of a ministerial recognition committee and had plenty of experience in talking to people considering ministry. Rob later became Principal of Regent's Park College, Oxford, which is one of the British Baptist colleges, where the major part of his job is training ministers.

Starting the process of discernment, I wrote to Roger Hayden, the Western Area Baptist General Superintendent; the equivalent of a Bishop in the Anglican church. He visited me and we talked. He was clear it was a confidential conversation and a few days later I received a letter giving his response to me. He told me that Ian had married a mathematician, not a minister, and he would not be able to cope with the change. That got Ian's back up as Ian was of the view that he had married me, not my career, and that Roger Hayden was making an incorrect assumption about someone he had not met. Ian has always been completely supportive of me. Despite my lecturing experience and acting as personal tutor to students, Roger Hayden told me I could not have a call because I did not have experience in preaching or pastoral care. Finally he said I was sick in body, mind and spirit and this was not the time to make changes. He left the door slightly ajar by adding that I could get in touch again in two years if I wanted to. I was shocked at the severity of his response and got in touch with Rob. I was horrified to discover that Rob was expecting me to contact him as Roger Hayden had sent him a copy of the letter that he had sent to me. I had assumed that when Roger had said our meeting was confidential that he meant it. I have since learnt that people are inclined to use the word confidential very loosely and rarely mean it as it is used in the Official Secrets Acts. I met again with Rob and knew this was not the end. I planned to continue lecturing maths until things became clearer.

By the time exams came round in the summer of 1988, I found I was given twice as much marking as anyone else. I had still been off sick when the January exams had been marked but was not expecting that load to be added to my marking in June. I do recall swearing when Professor Peregrine arrived in my office with about one hundred and fifty first year scripts that I had not realised were coming my way for marking. Annual staff reviews were just starting and I had to complete a form about my performance over the previous year and my plans for future years. As I filled in the form, I answered the question asking what I expected to achieve by the end of the following year by saying that I might no longer be in the department. I am sure those forms were simply filed away and not read because there was no response. The last straw came when my father informed me that Isabel was going to stay with her brother in Spain in September and that I would be looking after him for two weeks, ignoring the fact that I needed to prepare new courses and could not spare the time. There was no consultation with me. I was expected to be a dutiful daughter. I resigned my full-time tenured university lectureship uncertain what would happen next. I felt content and relieved.

Our year in Australia had upended my priorities in life. Now God came first, then family and finally work, even if the work were to be church work. I set out on the new path that lay before me. I did not know where it would lead. There were so many possibilities. Perhaps there are other universes where there were other outcomes; universes where I regretted my decision to leave maths, universes where I returned to lecturing or, entering the realms of fantasy, maybe even a universe where I fully broke the gender barriers and became Archbishop of Canterbury or Pope. I kept travelling on putting one foot in front of the other.

10. Back to the Drawing Board

According to Plato in his work *The Republic*, written about 375 BCE, the first years of life should be devoted to mathematics and only after the mathematical disciplines have been fully absorbed is it time to proceed to study philosophy. Admittedly this only applied to men, but I felt I was following Plato's advice when, at the age of thirty-four, I started a degree in theology at Bristol University, seventeen years after I had gone to Churchill. I had enjoyed my year out, taking some art and craft classes, as well as fulfilling a long-held desire to learn to play the flute. I decided to apply to Bristol Baptist College as an open-option student, reading for a theology degree for its own sake. I wanted to understand better what had happened to me in Australia, so it made sense to study the queen of sciences. Maths had lost its appeal. I arrived at my first lectures in the university to find Diarmaid MacCulloch teaching on the history of church architecture. I already knew Diarmaid, who had been the chapel organist at Churchill, and we had met a number of times at social functions in Bristol, so he was surprised when I turned up at his lectures. Diarmaid had been ordained as a deacon in the Church of England but had declined the possibility of priesthood when he was asked to deny his sexuality. It was not until after I left Cambridge that I discovered that Diarmaid, who had been a postgraduate and then a junior research fellow at Churchill, had been secretary to the Gay and Lesbian Christian Movement. At the time I would have been shocked to know that he was homosexual, having been told as a child that such things were unnatural. I no longer think that true. I find it more difficult to know that he was told by the church that it was fine to have a same-sex partner as long as he did not let anyone know. Honesty and integrity both seem to me to be essential to a godly life.

I really enjoyed studying theology, learning about Indian religions as well as Biblical studies, ethics, philosophy, New Testament Greek and Hebrew. There were two other students from the Baptist college, a number of Methodist student ministers and some other independent mature students taking the same course as me. The rest of the students were eighteen year olds, straight from school, and not all were well-motivated. I had thought theology students would have made a positive decision to study the subject, rather than just drifting into it because they were good at it at school, which is often the reason students have decided to study maths. However I found that the most popular reason for choosing to study theology at Bristol was that it was easier to get in to than English and that they had friends also coming to Bristol. Wanting to understand faith was rarely a motivation with the younger students, and I know that I would have found it too difficult to take a course that challenged my beliefs at that age. There was one first-year student who came from a Christian fundamentalist background and she failed to be able to cope with being able to look at things from a perspective other than her own. She left after the first year. There was a good gender balance on the course, which was a pleasant change from university-level maths, simply because it seemed like a better reflection of everyday life. On graduation the students not training for the ministry often took similar career paths to the maths students I had known, with a surprising number training as accountants.

As well as studying in the university, I was also attached to Bristol Baptist College, founded in 1679. It is the oldest Baptist college in the world. The student body here was largely evangelical Baptist so I appreciated the contrast that I found in the university. The majority of college students were taking courses taught by the two full-time college tutors and the principal, so most led an enclosed life within the college. During my first year I again went to see Roger Hayden, with a view to becoming a ministerial student. He had told me not to contact him for two years after our first meeting so I arrived in fear and trembling. This time he was sweetness and light and gave me the necessary forms to apply to the ministerial recognition committee without further interrogation. He told me that he always tried to put people off at first contact. I felt his approach was extreme but I did then proceed through the process without falling at further hurdles. I started my second year as a ministerial student. I was one of two women, out of a total of six ministerial students in my year, and by my final year we were the only two female ministerial students in college, out of a total of twenty. Baptists have been ordaining women as ministers since the 1920s but the proportion was still low. There have been Baptist women preachers since the denomination was formed back in the seventeenth century but a few local churches would not accept women. As students we went out most Sundays during term to preach around Bristol and South Wales. On the preaching plan my name appeared as Dr Holyer, which did not give away my gender, but I did manage to avoid going to any churches where I would not be welcome. There was a national grouping of female Baptist ministers which I only went to once, when I was still a student. They saw themselves as an embattled minority and I could not cope with their level of complaint, which seemed quite over the top to me. I was leapt upon for suggesting that there were other areas of work where the proportion of women was even lower.

The summer vacations included placements to help with our training. The first summer I spent ten weeks attached to Victoria Park Baptist Church, south of the river in Bristol, and took part in the daily life of a traditional church, including helping with its children's holiday club. The second summer I spent at the hospice; with two weeks working as a care assistant to the inpatients, two weeks at the day centre and two weeks travelling with the nurses to visit patients at home. I learnt a lot from both of these placements, especially the one at the hospice. On arriving at a doorstep, the open question, 'How are things?' worked much better than alternatives that enquired about the health of the patient. I started to learn to listen carefully, both to what was said and to what was left unsaid. The hospice placement was made more poignant by the continuing deterioration of my father's health.

Just after I had started at college my Auntie Edwina, now in her late eighties. started to be unable to care for herself as vascular dementia took hold. My father was her next of kin, with myself and my brother as her only other living relations. My father could not travel and my brother was rarely in the UK, so it fell to me to help to find the best care that I could for my aunt. I travelled over to Pontypridd as often as possible and, with the help of her neighbour and Social Services, we found a residential home where she settled. Fortunately she had agreed to giving me financial power of attorney before the move, so I could pay her bills. I visited fairly regularly, sometimes with Ian. She usually recognised me but had some trouble with Ian. 'Who is he?' she would ask with alarming regularity and we would remind her of our wedding in Cambridge. She did remember it and would say, 'Ooh! It was lovely,' in her lilting Welsh accent, but five minutes later she would again ask, 'Who is he?' She sometimes spoke of wanting to go home, but the house she spoke of was the house in which she had grown up, not the house she had been living in for the past fifty years. I would take along old photos for her and she would tell me who was who but she had no recollection of the present. It was clear she would not be returning home and I put her house on the market at Easter 1990 in order to be able to continue to pay her care home fees. I accepted an offer quite quickly and, having exchanged contracts, we were just about ready to complete when I received a phone call from the home to say that she had had a stroke and was in Dewi Sant hospital. Ian and I both went over to see her and it did not seem too severe. It looked as though she would recover. I arranged for the completion of the sale of her house for the following week, just before my first year theology exams were about to start. I had to drive over to sign the papers and it almost went according to plan, apart from the car breaking down on the way. As I drove along the motorway north of Cardiff, something happened in the automatic gearbox and the speed dropped abruptly to thirty miles an hour, which is not a good speed for the motorway. The car limped into Pontypridd, parked in the hospital car park and I went first to the solicitor's offices to sign the contract and then I visited my aunt, who had improved since the weekend and was sitting up in a chair. As evening approached, I had to wait for the AA breakdown van to arrive and, as the car could not be fixed on the spot, it was put on a truck and I was relayed back to Bristol, arriving at about 10pm. It was fun trying to explain to the driver that I had a New Testament exam the following morning. He had scarcely heard of the bible. The next day I made it through the exam, making occasional additional notes to myself about the house sale and practical things that I still needed to do. I hoped that I could now concentrate on the exams but a week later, walking into the house on a Thursday afternoon after a history exam, there was a call from the hospital. Auntie Edwina had had a second stroke and was not expected to survive. I waited until the following morning to take the train over to Pontypridd. The car was still not fixed. Taking texts by Plato and Descartes with me, I hoped that I might be able to prepare for the philosophy exam on Monday. When I arrived Auntie Edwina seemed to be unconscious and was breathing heavily but I greeted her and placed a chair so I could sit beside her. Since the previous evening I had had the last verse of a Charles Wesley hymn going around my head, 'Finish then thy new creation, Pure and spotless let us be. Let us see thy great creation, Perfectly restored in thee: Changed from glory into glory, Till in heav'n we take our place, Till we cast our crowns before thee, Lost in wonder, love and praise.' As I finished speaking, my aunt smiled and everything went quiet. Very quiet. Deathly quiet. It took me a while to convince myself that she had stopped breathing. I am inclined to say that she had gone to glory. It was a beautiful way to die. I felt privileged to have been given the words that brought her peace. So during my first theology exams I organised the funeral of my great aunt. I was not in a fit state for the philosophy exam. Several people, including the lecturer, asked me if I was alright but it was the last exam of the year and I got through it.

I never enjoyed theology exams. They were the most uncreative exercise I could imagine, as the essay questions were predictable and simply required regurgitation of prepared, memorised material that gave me cramp in my hands from trying to keep my handwriting legible. There was no possibility of checking sources, which was an essential feature of theology as the views of different writers were compared. Maths exams had required creativity as we attacked previously unseen problems in a restricted period of time where we had to decide which method was most appropriate. Of course my complaints of theology exams were not helped by my personal situation. By my third year exams my father was in hospital with an enormous pressure sore that was too deep to heal. I was not quite prepared for the question on the applied ethics paper that asked, 'When is it justifiable to consider that someone else's life is not worth living? Discuss with reference to...' I could only think of my father. I must have stared at the question for half an hour, contemplating walking out of the exam, before I managed to turn the paper over to answer a question on just war theory, when I could regurgitate my essay on nuclear weapons. I enjoyed writing essays during the year more, when I could use a computer for the word-processing and could think about what I was writing. I understand that the department does now use continuous assessment without exams. I did manage to replace one of the exams in my third year with an extended essay in Reformation studies. With the title, 'Continuity and Discontinuity between the Medieval Mystics and the

Spirituals of the Radical Reformation', it helped me to understand how mystical religion had not died with the Reformation. I guess that it was a decent piece of work because it was published in the Journal of the Baptist Historical Society.

At the end of my three years of theology I arranged to make a thirty day silent retreat as an antidote to all the academic theology that was swirling around my mind. The previous summer I had trained in Ignatian spirituality with Gerry Hughes and Graham Chadwick at Llys Fasi in North Wales, where I had discovered the mystical side of the Roman Catholic faith, kept safe by the Jesuit community. My original plan for the thirty day retreat was to go to St Beuno's, where the poet, Gerard Manley Hopkins, had spent some happy years, but its Gothic style reminded me too much of the Baptist College in Bristol. When Graham Chadwick suggested I could go instead to Mairead Quigley at Llannerchwen I said, 'Pardon.' After I had found out how to spell the names he had given me, and discovered that Llannerchwen was just north of Brecon, I decided to go there instead. The retreat was hard work but rewarding. I spent many hours each day in prayer and was expected to end each time of prayer with an imaginative conversation with God, Jesus and Mary. Now Mary is not prominent in Baptist life, seen only at Christmas in the traditional manger scenes. For a long time I could not manage the conversations with her, until one day, as I prayed, a drawing that I had blu tacked over a picture fell off. It was covering a rather sentimental picture of Mary. As it fell, I imagined Mary saying, 'That may be a bloody awful picture of me but it is a reminder that I am here.' In Mary, I found a strong and supportive woman, who is clearly also a part of me, and she makes an excellent replacement mother.

The retreat ended on 31st August 1992, August Bank Holiday Monday. I had gone away knowing my father's health was precarious but he was happy for me to go and I knew that Ian could contact me in an emergency. He picked me up from Llannerchwen and we had a pleasant day walking in the Brecon

Beacons before driving home. That night our phone rang at 4 am. It was the hospital calling, suggesting that it might be a good idea to come over to Swansea. My father died in the early hours of 1st September 1992 and I arrived an hour too late. My stepmother had already gone home. I sat with his body for half an hour, in a state of shock, and the nurses gave me a cup of tea before I went up to what was now Isabel's home. Before I had got in the door she asked me if I had ever ministered to someone who had just been bereaved. She never noticed that it was my father who had died and that I was bereaved too. She only cared that her husband of seven years had died. I again found myself having to arrange a funeral, fulfilling Isabel's wishes, and being told how lucky I was to have just had a long holiday. It took me a long time to process my father's death.

I was ordained on 29th October 1992 as a minister of the Baptist Union of Great Britain. I joined the chaplaincy team at the University of Bristol, as half-time Free Church Chaplain, and became part-time minister of Tytherington Baptist Church, a small church north of Bristol. I was able to choose the hymns for my ordination service and among others chose a hymn written by John Bell of the Iona Community, 'Will you come and follow me if I but call your name? Will you go where you don't know and never be the same?' It expressed how I felt about my new vocation, which I believed was God's call on my life. To my delight, the chaplaincy team was ecumenical and included two Anglicans, Angela Berners-Wilson and Jonathan Clark; a Roman Catholic, Edward Crouzet; two independent ministers, Rob Scott Cook and David Mitchell; an Orthodox priest, Kyril Leret; a Methodist, Peter Bishop; a United Reformed Church minister, Colin Baxter and Rob Ellis, the Baptist minister of Tyndale. For most of these people the chaplaincy work was very much part-time, as they were also running busy churches but I enjoyed working in a team where we could support each other. I asked Angela to participate in my ordination but she declined, as she did not want to do anything that might imply she was already a priest.

Instead I asked a student, the president of the injudiciously named BURC Soc, Liz Neal, who was happy to be part of a group laying hands on me. Bristol University has a number of society with odd names. The Baptist and United Reformed Church Society did not have quite as unfortunate a name as the music society, known as BUMS.

At the time of my ordination I was attending a course of lectures on patristics, the works of the early church fathers. These were given by Rowan Williams, who was then Bishop of Monmouth. One of the subjects covered was apostolic succession, where the ministry of the Christian church is seen as existing as the continuous succession of bishops, each going back to at least one of the apostles. I discovered that the succession of the Bishop of Monmouth is traditionally said to go back to Joseph of Arimathea, who was supposed to have come to Britain bringing Jesus with him in the years before Jesus's ministry began; the story that inspired William Blake's 'Jerusalem'. Apostolic succession is not part of Baptist theology. There are no Baptist bishops, just ministers who serve the church. Nevertheless, I was amused that one of the group that laid hands on me at my ordination, the URC minister, Colin Baxter, had been ordained in Guildford where the Bishop of Guildford had laid hands on him. I like the idea that I can claim to be part of the succession that is traditionally claimed to go back to the first apostles. I did invite Rowan and the other students of the patristics course to my Baptist ordination. Unfortunately Rowan was unable to come due to a confirmation service elsewhere. I have already mentioned the fiftieth anniversary of Churchill College Chapel when Rowan spoke of the chapel as a place where honesty is possible. I did not mention that that service was held on the 29th October 2017, the exact 25th anniversary of my ordination. To have Rowan preach on my silver anniversary was particularly gratifying. It was as if it were especially for me and it made up for him not being able to come to my ordination. He had not known of my connection to Churchill so was surprised to see me in the vestry before the service. Over the years I have met him from time to time at lectures and conferences and am always surprised that he remembers me. We do have a Swansea connection. The school I attended, Llwyn-y-bryn, amalgamated with the school he attended, Dynevor, in 1978, after we had both left, so I assume their was some similarity in our education. His memory of me may also relate to the badger glove puppet that I used to take to his lectures. It became a visual aid to explain the heresy of docetism, where Jesus is seen as a puppet in the hand of God rather than fully human and fully divine. Perhaps it was the cuddly toy that made me memorable. At the service in 2017, we spoke of the lectures he had given in Bristol twenty-five years earlier. I found myself saying that I did not believe in the existence of priests, who represent the people to God, unless it is seen as the priesthood of all believers. As far as I am concerned I have always been a minister and not a priest. It is not a conversation that I often get into and having it with a former Archbishop of Canterbury would at some points in church history have been not just imprudent but life-threatening. Fortunately Rowan took it in his stride. Perhaps honesty is possible in the church!

In 1992 I found myself in many debates on the ordination of women. My colleague, Angela Berners-Wilson, was keen that I did not preside at any communion services, in solidarity with her and other women who were seeking priesthood. I did not always comply with her wish. My church in Tytherington was in a local ecumenical project with the Anglicans and on Christmas eve I presided at communion with the Anglican priest at the parish church. This was allowed because I was an ordained minister and our churches were in a formal relationship. I could not deny my calling. Some people recall me saying at a seminar in the theology department that I did not believe that women had a right to be priests. They did not remember that I also said that I did not believe that men had a right to be priests. As far as I was concerned the arguments should not have been based on rights. If

God was calling women to the priesthood the church should never have stood in their way. I was pleased when the Church of England finally agreed in November 1992 that it would ordain women as priests, although it did cause the press to descend on Angela, who was the first woman in the United Kingdom to be ordained as priest in the Church of England in March 1994. The phone perpetually rang in the chaplaincy centre with journalists trying to find her, but I carefully never gave my name as Reverend Dr Judy Holyer, my correct title, as I did not want the press chasing me too.

As I settled into my new role as a Baptist minister, I started getting flashbacks to my childhood and events that I half forgotten and only half remembered. On the whole I do remember the events that have formed my life very well, especially those of my adult life, but it seems that I had been using my academic abilities to squash memories that I could not cope with. By September, a year after my father's death, I was starting to piece things together and it was traumatic as things returned to consciousness. I got in touch with David Cook, the consultant, that I had seen back in 1987 when I had the breakdown. I arranged to see him, hoping he would be able stop the emotional pain that I was no longer able to avoid. There was a line in the hymn from the 'Will you come and follow me?' from my ordination that almost haunted me. 'Will you love the 'you' you hide if I but call your name? Will you quell the fear inside and never be the same?' It took me a very long time to tell David Cook that I feared that I had been sexually abused by both of my parents, with my mother's violations dominating my memories. I could barely speak and would shake uncontrollably as I tried to verbalise things that had previously only existed as pictures in my mind. I felt guilty at what I was remembering. I hoped he would tell me I was imagining it all, perhaps locking me up until I came to my senses. His reaction was that everything I was telling fitted with what he already knew of me and that he should have realised earlier that I had been abused. He did not see any signs of mental illness. As my first year as a chaplain ended there was a national conference of university chaplains held at High Leigh in Hertfordshire. Rob Ellis and I drove there together and as we drove along the motorways to our destination I told him of the problems I was having with flashbacks. It was easier to talk in a car than face-to-face. I did not want him to see the fear in my eyes. As I talked I realised that what was causing me problems was reality. It was TS Eliot in the Four Quartets who wrote that humankind cannot bear very much reality. I was running the book room at the conference, selling books that other people had brought with them. John Bell had come from Glasgow, with two suitcases full of Iona community publications, and so I got to meet the author of my favourite hymn. He was there to lead the worship. The final worship session was intended to be a quiet meditative session where the hundred or so chaplains, sitting around a table, were invited to reflect on the significant events of their lives, starting with infancy, lighting candles in memory or prayer as the worship continued. It was unfortunate that I had placed myself a long way from the only exit, because I found myself shaking in fear as I struggled with the reality of flashbacks and I sat with my head down and eyes shut. The session was immediately followed by dinner but I could not bring myself to talk to anyone, so I took myself into the grounds where I dined on the blackberries growing in the less accessible parts of the garden. Eventually returning to the house, I locked myself into the book room where I needed to balance the books and work out what money was due to whom. It was with relief that I discovered that the first person knocking on the door was Rob, who had registered that the worship session had upset me and had sought me out. He told me that many people, including himself, had found the worship moving in a helpful way but could also clearly see that it had not been helpful to me. The second person who came that night was John Bell, to whom I owed a lot of money as the books he had brought had sold very well. I did not hold the worship session against him and we chatted. Even though I was not in a place where I could look at my parents in thankfulness, I still recognised that it was helpful to some. It was probably a good thing that I had spoken to Rob first. John Bell gave me two copies of books of his music, which he signed for me, and I told him how much I liked his hymn, 'Will you come and follow me?' He did manage to make me laugh by telling me about the wedding of some friends of his. They had chosen the same hymn, perhaps because its author was one of the guests, but it does not work well as a wedding hymn, bringing up visions of a man with a subservient wife trailing behind him.

In writing this memoir I have been very uncertain what I should say of the abuse I suffered, which was largely at the hands of my mother. I am not going to go into details. It is easy to write in a way that becomes voyeuristic and there is more to my life than the abuse. I spent many years seeing a therapist once a week and painfully slowly I have learnt to stop blaming myself for what happened and to accept my feelings. It feels as if I had to rebuild my life from its foundations. I had stopped crying when I was four, after one particular incident with my mother, and had not cried again until my baptism in Australia almost thirty years later. My mother's view was that women cried to manipulate situations and violently objected to my crying. If you are hit often enough for something, you learn not to do it. Now I made up for the lost years and I discovered a whole wealth of nuances to emotions that I had not needed during my mathematical career. I am not a great fan of the concept of hell but for many years I indulged myself with the thought that this was where my parents were, in separate solitary confinement. Now I tend to think they were the victims of the circumstances of their own lives and it would be appropriate to quote a poem by Philip Larkin about parents, except that I do not want to swear. If you do not know the poem, then look it up. There is no excuse for how my parents treated me. They were the responsible adults. I survived by living in my mind and school was a safe place away from home, where I could thrive.

My stepmother lived until she was ninety-eight, dying in 2017, twenty-five years after the death of my father. She idolised my father and the house in Swansea was almost like a shrine to his memory. She had resented her first husband, who she blamed for their childlessness. It has only been since her death that I have been able to look back at my life with any sense of perspective. I am finally free of the pain that my childhood caused me.

The twenty-five years between my father's death and my stepmother's have not been empty. But it is time to draw this memoir to a close. I feel as if I have said most of what I need to say. If I spent all my time writing down the things that I do and have done there would be no time left to actually live. It occurs to me that I am not the only author to have had this problem. Saint John ends his gospel with the words, 'There are also many other things which Jesus did, which if they would all be written, I suppose that even the world itself wouldn't have room for the books that would be written.' I do not need to say everything that could be said.

11. Not the End

I enjoy sitting in coffee shops watching the world go by and pondering. I look at other people and wonder if I am normal. Then I wonder if I want to be normal. I want to be myself, connected to others, but accepting that we all have different interests and needs. Like everyone's life, my life is unique. I am not easily pigeon-holed. I do not think labels work well on anyone. I like things to be fluid. I would like to say that I am a flâneuse, living in the city and observing all around me. My husband usually says that I am a polymath, interested in everything. Job titles leave me cold. They do not tell me who someone is, just what role they are filling at a particular time in their life. I now consider myself retired from work but I have not retired from life. People will sometimes ask what I did before I retired, as if that would define me. It does not. I am me. What do I do? I live.

I feel that popular feminism has done most women no favours. It does not help to define certain characteristics as female and others as male. Neither women nor men constitute a single homogeneous group. Nurturing is not the sole monopoly of men. Power is not the sole monopoly of women. Some men like to wear dresses. Some women like to wear trousers. Sexual abuse and harassment are not solely perpetrated by men, as I know to my cost. I have no interest in make-up or fashion. My husband has no interest in football or cars. I have no idea why there still seems to be a prevalent idea in our society that it is somehow masculine to study science, especially when it is put alongside the idea that women cannot do science because is is logical and rational. Science itself shows this not to be true. Iain McGilchrist writes in his erudite exposition of the brain, *The Master and His Emissary: The Divided Brain and the Making of the Western World*, of the absurd popular misconception that the left hemisphere, hard-nosed and logical, is somehow male, and the right hemisphere, dreamy and sensitive, is somehow female. He goes on to say, 'If there is any evidence that could begin to associate each sex with a single cerebral hemisphere in this way, it tends to indicate, if anything, the reverse.' Cambridge University as a whole now admits as many women as men but Churchill College does not. The requirement that the college must admit 70% scientists seems to be generally cited as the reason for this. To me, it is a sad reflection of a society where it is seen as strange for women to be scientists. Physical sciences are a great subject for anyone to study. The numbers need to increase not because of women's rights but because science is fun and worthwhile. The current situation does no-one any favours. I look forward to the day when there are equal numbers of male and female nurses and primary school teachers, as well as research scientists.

I am grateful to the fellows of Churchill College, all male, who agreed in 1969 to make the necessary changes to the college statutes so that women could be admitted. They had the sense to know that the college was losing out by excluding half the population because of its gender. Men and women are not so very different and denying education to women was wrong. I like the idea that the fellows of Churchill wanted the college to admit women because their intelligence was needed by society and should not be allowed to go to waste. I thrived in the environment I found there. Churchill College was founded to improve the industrial base of the country and I do like to think I have played my part both in my research and teaching. At the newly founded Topexpress Ltd I had worked on national security issues and I jointly founded an IT company, Degree2 Innovations, in 1999. By going to Churchill my horizons were broadened and I found a freedom to live that I had not previously known. My intellectual curiosity has never abated. Universities grew out of the scholastic education of monasteries and, back in 11th century Paris, Hugh of St Victor wrote, 'Learn all you can. You will find later that nothing is ever wasted.' It is advice that I still follow.

As I end my ramblings, the motto of Churchill College comes to mind, 'Forward.' It is taken from Winston Churchill's first speech to the House of Commons when he became prime minister, 'Come, then, let us go forward together.' I like that quote because we are all united by our common humanity. Our journeys continue ever onward. Life goes on. My life is now much simpler. The existentialist philosopher, Søren Kierkegaard, wrote in his journal that life can only be understood backwards but can only be lived forwards. As I look back on the maze of twisty passages of my life, it is still hard to see the map. I do not know where the exit is or how long it will take me to reach it. I just plan to carry on living life to the full and when I find the exit I hope to gracefully move forward to find my place in God's never-ending future.

Acknowledgements

Finally I owe thanks to many people. Firstly I would like to thank Professor Mark Goldie of Churchill College who persuaded me that I was able to fill a gap in the college history by writing of my experiences of coming to college as one of its first women. According to him, everyone ought to write a memoir, if only to help future historians. He has been a great encouragement to me and without him this book would not have come into existence.

Secondly I would like to thank everyone who has helped in the writing and production of this book; particularly Colin Dalton, Sue Marsden, David Probert, Margaret Silf, Richard Trouncer and Michael Whitfield. There are others but the list might get too long. If you feel your name should have been included, then take it as read that I thank you too. All views and opinions expressed are entirely my own.

Most importantly my thanks go to my husband, Ian. I owe him more than words can express. He is my support and helpmeet in all things.

About the Book

Judith Probert arrived at Churchill College, Cambridge, in 1972 as one of its first female undergraduates. This is her thoughtful and, at times, poignant memoir. Part of her story is shocking but she was and remains a survivor.

She brings a refreshing look at life in Cambridge, where, while studying mathematics to a high level, she met many well-known people, including two successive Lucasian professors, James Lighthill and Stephen Hawking. After obtaining a doctorate in fluid dynamics, she became a Junior Research Fellow at Girton College and also worked as a research scientist at Topexpress Ltd, a university start-up company. In 1981 she moved to Bristol to take up a lectureship in mathematics at the university. After seven years lecturing and a trip to Australia, her world turned upside down and she changed career, training as a Baptist minister and acquiring a second BA, this time in theology. After ordination Judy became Free Church Chaplain to Bristol University and later Baptist Chaplain at the University of the West of England. Finally she embarked on a third career, co-founding a tech start-up company, Degree2 Innovations, for which she co-created the patents. Now retired she has become a Quaker and leads a quiet, contemplative life in Bristol.

Judy is married to Ian Holyer, a contemporary from Churchill College, who lectures in computer science at Bristol University.

36492014R00107

Printed in Poland
by Amazon Fulfillment
Poland Sp. z o.o., Wrocław